YOU ARE A
CURSE
BREAKER

Books by Jennifer Eivaz

The Intercessors Handbook
Seeing the Supernatural
Glory Carriers
Prophetic Secrets
Inner Healing and Deliverance Handbook
Awaken the Dreamscape
You Are a Cursebreaker

"*You Are a Cursebreaker* is a clarion call to every believer standing at the intersection of generational pain and prophetic promise. Jennifer Eivaz exposes the schemes of ancestral bondage and equips readers to break cycles, redeem bloodlines, and walk boldly in spiritual freedom. This book is both timely and timeless—a must-read for those called to shift their family legacy."

Rev. Samuel Rodriguez, lead pastor, New Season Church; president, NHCLC; author, *Persevere with Power*

"Jennifer Eivaz leads you along the process of walking out your breakthrough—not just as a single moment in time but as a new lifestyle, empowered by the Holy Spirit. This book is hard to put down because of its compelling testimonies, scriptural insights, and clear applications for believers today. I highly recommend it if you want to see greater levels of breakthrough in your life and the lives of those around you."

Dr. Ché Ahn, senior leader, Harvest Rock Church, Pasadena, CA; president, Harvest International Ministry; international chancellor, Wagner University

"This book is for those who know they were born to break cycles and release blessings into their family line. Jennifer Eivaz has given the Body of Christ a manual filled with wisdom, spiritual authority, and prophetic insight. *You Are a Cursebreaker* will help you identify what's been holding your family back—and how to uproot it. Quietly but powerfully, the spirit of Elijah moves through these pages to bring family restoration where it's most needed."

Apostle John Eckhardt, Crusaders Church Chicago

"Prophetic voice Jennifer Eivaz leads us in a journey of biblical empowerment, deliverance, and inner healing. This is a how-to manual for walking in freedom from familiar spirits and other life-controlling issues. You will be enlightened and inspired to see the purpose of God established in your life and in the lives of the people you love."

Dr. Kynan Bridges, pastor and bestselling author; president, Kynan Bridges Ministries, Inc.

"*You Are a Cursebreaker* is a courageous, Spirit-led call to rise up and be the first in your family to walk in freedom. Many desire freedom but feel frustrated that they just can't seem to get there. Jennifer Eivaz writes with clarity, compassion, and prophetic insight—equipping a generation to confront generational strongholds and restore their bloodline in Christ."

Banning Liebscher, founder, Jesus Culture; pastor and author

"Extraordinary. Exceptional. Remarkable. And absolutely supernatural. This book took my understanding of stubborn strongholds to an entirely new level. Through powerful real-life stories and vivid illustrations, Jen communicates her insights with clarity and conviction. She even guides readers through complex, and sometimes controversial, issues—like the distinction between declarations and decrees. Prepare yourself for a life-changing journey. As you read, you'll welcome the profound revelation: You are a cursebreaker. And yes, you really are."

Bishop Dave Williams, DMin, DD, founder, American Center for Pacesetting Leadership

"Jennifer Eivaz courageously shares her own journey out of generational strongholds and then expertly guides you, step by step, into those same breakthroughs. This meaty, deep-dive handbook unpacks every dimension of cursebreaking—from personal and family bonds to regional and territorial strongholds—and equips you with biblical decrees to apply in your own life. It's our privilege to recommend *You Are a Cursebreaker* to anyone seeking true freedom and breakthrough for themselves, their loved ones, and their communities."

Ben and Jodie Hughes, Pour It Out Ministries; authors, *When God Breaks In* and *The King's Decree*

"*You Are a Cursebreaker* has incredible insight and keys to help you and your family walk in the freedom we are called to walk in. Jennifer's powerful testimony and examples give real authority in the area of discernment and deliverance because she doesn't just speak from head knowledge. She has walked it out in her personal life and extended that same grace to bring freedom to so many others. Her testimonies will stir your faith to know Jesus more and to truly experience the freedom that He purchased for us to walk in!"

Michael and Meredith Mauldin, founders, UPPERROOM (Dallas) music label and publishing and SongLab; authors, *It's All About Worship*

YOU ARE A CURSE BREAKER

SHATTER GENERATIONAL CURSES AND CLAIM SPIRITUAL BLESSINGS

JENNIFER EIVAZ

Chosen

a division of Baker Publishing Group
Minneapolis, Minnesota

Published by Chosen Books
Minneapolis, Minnesota
ChosenBooks.com

Chosen Books is a division of
Baker Publishing Group, Grand Rapids, Michigan

Printed in the United States of America

Library of Congress Cataloging-in-Publication Data
Names: Eivaz, Jennifer author
Title: You are a cursebreaker : shatter generational curses and claim spiritual
    blessings / Jennifer Eivaz.
Description: Minneapolis, Minnesota : Chosen, a division of Baker Publishing
    Group, [2026]
Identifiers: LCCN 2025014844 | ISBN 9780800762155 paperback | ISBN
    9780800778422 casebound | ISBN 9781493452934 ebook
Subjects: LCSH: Blessing and cursing—Biblical teaching
Classification: LCC BS680.B5 E573 2026 | DDC 235/.4—dc23/eng/20250813
LC record available at https://lccn.loc.gov/2025014844

Cover design by InsideOut Creative Arts, Inc.

Baker Publishing Group publications use paper produced from sustainable forestry practices and postconsumer waste whenever possible.

26 27 28 29 30 31 32   7 6 5 4 3 2 1

I dedicate this book to my Lord and Savior, Jesus Christ—
the Supreme Cursebreaker, the Restorer of all things, and
the faithful Preserver of families and generational blessings.
To Him be all glory, honor, and praise.

CONTENTS

Foreword by Dr. Michael Maiden   13

Introduction: Setting Free the Family Tree   15

1. Ancestral Spirits, Druids, and the Familiar   21
    Ensnared by Ancestral Spirits
    Have Nothing in Common
    Who Are the Druids?
    The Occult Grips Families Until Deliverance
    Familiar Spirits Will Stop the New
    Breaking the Cycle of Familiar Spirits

2. Understanding Strongmen and Strongholds   39
    Bind the Strongman
    Can a Christian Be Possessed?
    The Power of Inner Healing and Deliverance
    Strongholds Take Time to Dismantle
    From the Personal to the Territorial

3. You'll Break Through in This Generation   55
    Hope to Heal Ancestral Chains
    The Weight of Unresolved Issues
    The Mystery of Iniquity
    The Roots of Iniquity

Contents

Corrupted Bloodlines Were Destroyed
The Season of Fulfillment
The Fight for Promises
Confronting the Jebusites
A Generational Shift

4. When You're the First to Break Free   71
Dying to Go Forward
The Holy Spirit's Call to "Transitional People"
God Gives You Strength for the Turnaround
God Sees Your Family, Past to Future
The Warrior Within: Leaving a Legacy
People of Repentance—Removing Legal Ground
Start Breaking Curses

5. The Power to Restore a Family Bloodline   87
Reclaim Your Spiritual Heritage
From the Tongue to Reality
Declare and Decree: Do You Know the Difference?
The Supernatural Force of Decrees
When Decrees Shift Destinies
Decreeing God's Will, Not Personal Agendas
Decrees to Transform Your Family

6. Here Comes the New   103
The Breakthrough Principle
The Prophetic Power of Your Breakthrough
New Wine, New Thinking, New Things
Discerning an Opportunity in the New
Stepping into Greater Works
Stepping into Global Ministry Now
The Perez Principle in Families
Shattering Ceilings Is Your Assignment

7. Fight for Your Marriage   119
Marriage: God's Original Blueprint
Marriage as Covenant: The Sacred Union

Faithfulness Is More Than Not Cheating

When Pride Takes Root, Love Fails

The Spirit of Elijah Prevents a Curse

Elijah Versus the Spirit of Jezebel

Guarding What Is Sacred

8. Breaking the Curse Brings Economic Revival   135

Secret Oaths, Symbols, and Spiritual Ties

The Layers of Darkness

Incredibly Dark

Healing the Land

From Barren to Blessed

The Land Remembers

Repentance Is the Divine Reset Button

Sick Land, Sick Body

When the Land Is Blessed, Everything Changes

Epilogue: You Were Made for This   153

Acknowledgments   155

Appendix A: Breaking Free from Generational Druidism   157

Appendix B: We Decree the New   163

Notes   167

FOREWORD

Jennifer Eivaz has a powerful personal testimony of how the Lord has helped her break curses in her life, overcoming them by prayer, perseverance, and faith. This testimony, coupled with the powerful prophetic mantle she carries, makes her a reliable, trustworthy carrier of this message.

I can't think of anyone in this generation who is more qualified and more capable of giving us this treasured resource you hold in your hands than Jennifer.

In *You Are a Cursebreaker*, Jennifer has written an incredibly timely, powerful, and insightful book—an in-depth spiritual manual on breaking curses.

As the enemy continues to unleash great deception upon humankind, this book will be a literal guide to recognizing and overcoming the enemy's strategies unleashed upon our lives, family, and world.

God wants you free! Allow the deep spiritual insights and revelations you will find in these pages to guide you to the freedom Jesus died to give you!

Dr. Michael Maiden, senior pastor,
Church for the Nations, Phoenix, Arizona

INTRODUCTION

Setting Free the Family Tree

In my life and ministry, I have experienced significant moments through divine revelations and prophetic utterances. One such encounter happened with Dr. Michael Maiden, founder and senior leader of Church for the Nations in Phoenix, Arizona. His prophetic insight revealed a destiny for me intertwined with the supernatural workings of God, and it acknowledged my calling to equip and empower others in their prophetic giftings. Dr. Maiden's prophetic word vividly portrayed a scene of spiritual warfare and triumph, affirming my authority over darkness and my role in delivering people from deception. His vision also confirmed that God had strategically positioned me to declare both His Word and prophetic words, to dismantle strongholds in regions marked by spiritual oppression.

Dr. Maiden's words served not only as a prediction but also as a divine confirmation of my journey as a "breaker of curses" and a vessel chosen by God to bring forth a book that would set free the family tree. Dr. Maiden spoke these prophetic words to me at Harvest Church in Turlock, California, on November 20, 2022:

> It's in your heart, Jennifer, to train people to develop their prophetic gifts. This is a beautiful thing because God is punishing the devil. I saw something. I think it was either last night or the night before. I had a dream and watched God reach into a dark oppression and pull you out of it. You're a rescued one, a redeemed one, and a delivered one. God gave you authority over all the things He brought you out of.
>
> I saw occultic things and strong powers, as there has been such an unleashing of hellish oppression in mankind. God has powerfully equipped you to deliver the oppressed. You're a walking testimony of what God can do. You have the authority to deliver people from demonic deceptions. There will be radical deliverances. I saw a witch that would switch. All these things are and will happen, just one after another, through your ministry. The Lord is pleased with the way that you've taught the people. You represent a prophetic gift that loves the local church, and we need more of that.
>
> I saw the Lord. He had a map and began circling regions. You had the authority to declare a word in every region God sent you to. When you declared the word, it began to dismantle these dark powers. It's not an accident that you travel to the geographical places you travel to. *It has a heavenly purpose, as you are the breaker of curses.*

I didn't hear anything else after that. I heard him say "you are the breaker of curses," and he's right. I have spent my entire Christian life breaking curses, most of which were family curses. I will explain more about family curses and family blessings throughout this book. Family curses are not easily revealed. In other words, they do not announce themselves, and once they are identified, they do not go away without a fight. They also attempt to return repeatedly, and it requires vigilance to keep the doors shut. The beautiful thing is that once you have overcome a curse, you will continue to do so for others. You will become a curse identifier, counselor, and intercessor. What you have overcome, you will ultimately help remove from the lives of others again and again. I believe this brings great contentment to our heavenly Father, and I have experienced deep and personal satisfaction in bringing people out of their captivity, especially in the same areas I had been held captive in myself.

This book you hold in your hands was birthed in response to Dr. Maiden's prophetic word. We can receive inspiration from King Jehoshaphat's instructions to the Israelites. He counseled them to believe the words of God's prophets in order to prosper:

> So they rose early in the morning and went out into the Wilderness of Tekoa; and as they went out, Jehoshaphat stood and said, "Hear me, O Judah and you inhabitants of Jerusalem: Believe in the LORD your God, and you shall be established; believe His prophets, and you shall prosper."
>
> 2 Chronicles 20:20

When we encounter a prophecy and determine that those words truly came from the Holy Spirit, we must take appropriate action. I've written every one of my books in obedience to the leading of the Holy Spirit, and this book is no different. Its contents were purposed in heaven before coming forth in the earth.

Dr. Maiden knew some of my history, but only the highlights. What I believed to be my testimony was this: I had an alcoholic, schizophrenic, and sexually abusive father from Hollywood, California, whom I saw off and on between the ages of four and seventeen. I also grew up in the Mormon Church and later discovered significant familial connections with Freemasonry. There were sizeable gaps of time from my growing-up years that seemed to be missing, however, and I couldn't remember what had happened during these periods. I thought this was normal and never questioned it. When I turned forty-seven, my memories from those missing years finally surfaced in response to a profoundly transforming Holy Spirit encounter. Those memories involved some of my family members subjecting me to violent satanism, sorcery, and ritual rape. I was also trafficked within an occult pedophile network in Hollywood by my biological father, among other things.

My story followed a typical psychological pattern for all those who have survived this kind of horror, but it's a story not typically understood or even believed by those who have never experienced it. Although my story is extreme, I would describe my healing journey as both costly and time-consuming, and yet undoubtedly miraculous. God is very good and knows how to heal the worst of the worst. You can read more about this in my book *Inner Healing and Deliverance Handbook*.

My entire Christian life has been a journey and testimony of breakthroughs. Most, if not all, of my struggles were related to family curses. Whenever I mention the possibility of family curses, I am met with two very opposite extremes. Some people do not believe that Christians can be cursed, which they base on Galatians 3:13 (ESV), which reads, "Christ redeemed us from the curse of the law by becoming a curse for us." The idea is that God's judgment for our sin fell completely on Christ, and any idea of being cursed or living out a curse is ludicrous. Citing the promise and not the process, these people mistakenly believe that if Jesus paid the price, then all curses have been automatically eliminated. Legally this is true, but Satan doesn't let go easily. Most who adhere to this kind of thinking have not yet identified symptoms of the curse, such as sickness, poverty, insanity, etc., nor have they asked themselves on a practical level if they or any Christian whom they know has exhibited such symptoms.

Other people lack solid teaching about Christ's full redemption from curses. They also lack the knowledge of how to walk out their freedom in Him. Sadly, when symptoms hit, they become infatuated with deliverance remedies that are not grounded in Scripture and either don't work or don't last. They connect with unaccountable deliverance ministries that keep them in the spin cycle of lousy teaching and deliverance hype, ministries using spiritual methods that leave them worse and not better. One man was filmed being delivered from a demon by a popular deliverance minister. His "deliverance" not only was filmed in a public setting but also became a viral video on this minister's social media. The man ended up at our church, desperate and asking for help because he became worse and not better. Clearly, the methods used by the minister were ungrounded and achieved great social media press only. They did not bring any relief to this man.

My life is proof that wicked, stubborn curses can be broken, releasing tremendous blessings. I will discuss extensively in the pages ahead that there is a process involved between God's promises for freedom found in the Scriptures and actual breakthroughs. This book is filled with insight and understanding and will open your eyes not only to family curses but to your spiritual inheritance that God has assigned to your family tree. I pray and believe that reading this book will lead to a significant change in your world. Let's proceed together and break these curses, shall we?

ONE

Ancestral Spirits, Druids, and the Familiar

We were praying deeply for a gathering in Western Australia. Our fervent heart cry was this: *"Show us more of Your glory!"* The gathering was my second one like this in the nation and was designed for prophets, seers, prophetic dreamers, and those curious about the prophetic gift. God faithfully answered our prayer in a way that elevated my faith and changed my life forever. You see, at that gathering there was an exhibition of God's glory unlike anything I had ever experienced. It was so glorious that I needed wisdom and counsel afterward because I didn't know how to move past it.

I've since learned that it is tempting to camp around one experience from God, wanting to relive it over and over, deceptively believing that you'll never have a greater one. I found the best advice came from my husband, a man of deep faith and wisdom. Ron said, "Stay humble, because you didn't make that happen." He added, "At the same time, don't put limits on what God will do in the future, all based on what happened in the past. He will always do more than that."

My husband's words resonated deeply with me, reinforcing the lesson I had learned. What took place was this: The Holy Spirit spontaneously burst upon the attendees that first night in uproarious laughter. I had not seen this happen so strongly since the Rodney Howard-Browne "laughing" revival that took place while my husband and I were students at Oral Roberts University. This unusual revival took place in 1993 and became a notable revival element that emerged *hilariously* in many houses of worship around the globe during that time.

This controversial experience likely appears in the Bible during the Church's inception in Acts 2. The boisterous behavior of the saints baptized in the Holy Spirit in the Upper Room led the apostle Peter to explain to the gathering crowds, "For these are not drunk, as you suppose" (Acts 2:15). We also see a possible suggestion of it in Ephesians 5:18, which reads, "And do not be drunk with wine, in which is dissipation; but be filled with the Spirit." This suggests a sanctified and highly joyful expression for the believer, by the unction of the Holy Spirit. And finally, in 1 Peter 1:8 (KJV), we read about a Holy Spirit encounter with supernatural joy, described as "joy unspeakable and full of glory."

On our second night in Western Australia, attendees underwent a mass deliverance after I shared an unusual word for freedom that came from a dream. A mass deliverance is a type of deliverance from demons that is typically ministered to an entire group of people all at once, whereas in individual deliverance ministry one person at a time is ministered to. I had described to the crowd an encounter with a "thief of time" who appeared in my dream looking like a locust/wormlike creature. The Scripture that came to mind was this: "So I will restore to you the years that the swarming locust has eaten, the crawling locust, the consuming locust, and the chewing locust, My great army which I sent among you" (Joel 2:25).

Apparently, this dream-time creature I saw was some kind of territorial spirit, and God's remedy was to release an angel to restore the people's lost years. When I prayed for God to send His angel of restoration, many in the room expressed a deep and unprompted tribal-sounding moan. The sound that emerged is complex to describe; it was an unrehearsed sound that I had never heard before and have never heard since.

On the third night, there was an unusual miracle of glory during a "fire tunnel," a method used to easily release more individual prayer to more people. Ministry team members lined up in the front of the room facing one another, leaving enough space between them for attendees to walk through in single file. When people walked through the line, each team member laid hands on them while praying, saying words of blessing over them, and believing God's power to come strongly upon them.

A fire tunnel is usually very vibrant, and those who walked through the line that night exhibited deep spiritual manifestations due to being touched by the presence of God. Some would spontaneously laugh as if drunk, some would experience a noticeable spiritual ecstasy, and others found it hard to stand because the power of God was so strongly upon their person. While we were conducting the fire tunnel, a true miracle of glory took place. It began to rain noticeably inside the building. The rain was golden in color, including gold flakes falling on people and bursts of white feathers occurring in midair. Many people believe such bursts of white feathers to have an angelic origin.

This new level of God's glory was unlike anything the attendees or I had ever experienced. It wasn't just what you saw, but also what you felt. There was a pure, heavenly power that charged the atmosphere. God Himself had collectively marked us with a spectacular sign, but there was just one problem. . . .

Ensnared by Ancestral Spirits

I stepped out to minister deliverance, targeting ancestral spirits that had a grip on some of the conference attendees. The room was alive with a powerful mix of nations—Australian Indigenous, New Zealand Māori, Filipino, Samoan, Singaporean, Tongan, and more. What a stunning display of God's heart for the nations! But let's be real—many of these cultures were steeped in ancestral worship long before Jesus came into the picture. And those ancestral spirits? They don't just leave because you've switched teams. They have to be confronted, evicted, and sent packing in Jesus' name!

Ancestral spirits are demons and will attach themselves to families in the guise of deceased relatives. They are also known as *familiar spirits* or *family spirits*, and their goal is to control an entire bloodline for demonic purposes.

People ensnared by these spirits believe them to be the spirits or souls of deceased family members or ancestors. These spirits are deceptively seen as benevolent and supportive entities that can offer guidance, protection, blessings, or warnings to their living descendants. Living descendants believe they can honor and communicate with their ancestors through rituals, prayers, offerings, or ceremonies. This practice is common in many traditional and indigenous religions.

Worshiping your ancestors is the worship of demons, and it is an active form of the occult. Its practices are particularly binding within the family and hold tightly to each successive generation. Those who refuse to participate could suffer rejection and alienation at the hands of their family members as punishment. They also suffer spiritual punishment from hosting demons, until they are fully delivered.

The affected conference attendees were Christians at various levels of maturity, but I was confident that they were not worshiping their ancestors. Yet I knew in my spirit that many attendees were still bound to ancestral spirits for an unknown reason, and they could not get any breakthrough when I began ministering in prayer for freedom. While ministering to deal with this, I encountered one such spirit standing up proudly inside a man who was attempting to intimidate me. This incident told me that deliverance and freedom would take more than the traditional chain-breaking prayer I had effectively engaged in before. I also needed to have nothing in common with these spirits myself.

Have Nothing in Common

Since becoming a Christian, I have encountered personal deliverance battles from demonic spirits, all seemingly connected to my personal and family history and also to my calling in God. I'm a prophet to nations, an intercessor, and a deliverance minister. When I say that I'm a deliverance minister, I don't just bring deliverance to individuals from personal demons; I also work to bring regional deliverance, which is more about subduing territorial spirits who have blinded the eyes of unbelievers to the Gospel. As the apostle Paul put it in 2 Corinthians 4:4 (NLT), "Satan, who is the god of this world, has blinded the minds of those who don't believe. They are unable to see the glorious light of the Good News. They don't understand this message about the glory of Christ, who is the exact likeness of God."

Territorial spirits are widely believed to be ruling demons that control entire regions and nations, such as the demonic princes of Persia and Greece mentioned in Daniel 10:20, and what Paul referred to in Ephesians 6:12—namely the powers, principalities, rulers of darkness, and hosts of wickedness.[1] When the Holy Spirit calls me on assignment to a nation, I will target prevailing demonic strongholds that empower territorial spirits, and I will release the appropriate remedy. To execute this effectively requires the Holy Spirit's gift of discerning of spirits, wisdom, and counsel. At the same time, before I can subdue or lessen the impact of a territorial spirit, I must deal with any aspect I may have in common with it.

Jesus said Satan had nothing in Him: "The ruler of this world is coming, and he has nothing in Me" (John 14:30). We are also instructed in the Scriptures that light and darkness cannot mix, and righteousness and wickedness don't coexist: "Do not be yoked together with unbelievers. For what do righteousness and wickedness have in common? Or what fellowship can light have with darkness?" (2 Corinthians 6:14 NIV).

I've often discovered hidden personal or hereditary strongholds and demonic covenants that needed to be addressed and dismantled before I could become effective. For example, I have English ancestry. Before my first ministry trip to England, I knew I needed to receive targeted prayer ministry that addressed the hidden sins of my English forefathers, especially the occult involvement. Consider that you might not know what happened in your bloodline, but familiar spirits do know, and they don't forget. If a spiritual agreement your forefathers made has not been severed, demons and familiar spirits could become activated to come and collect on the spiritual debt from ensuing generations.

While receiving personal prayer ministry, I discovered a hidden area of commonality with a demonic order along this line. The prayer minister asked, "Do you have any Druids in your bloodline?" She asked this for two reasons. Those with European ancestry often have this somewhere in their family tree, and she also believed she had a word of knowledge, meaning the Holy Spirit supernaturally revealed a fact to her about my family's past.

I responded to her question with a strong "No, not at all."
She countered, "Are you sure?"
I replied, "I'm positive."

She went after it again and asked if we could pray around this area "just in case." I consented and, at her leading, began to repent of and renounce any generational covenants with druidism. It went something like this:

On behalf of my forefathers and mothers, I repent for any participation by my ancestors in druidic worship, sacrifices, or rituals. I renounce any hidden ancestral covenants with Druids and Druid practices, in the name of Jesus. . . .

When I prayed this, I shockingly and suddenly took on the appearance of a ghostlike apparition. You could see straight through me for about ten to fifteen minutes. Bloodline sorcery had been hidden in my life, the kind involving shape-shifting, and I had no idea it was there until I repented and renounced it. In biblical terms, shape-shifting refers to the ability of certain spiritual beings to change their outward appearance while remaining the same in essence. Satan, for example, is described in Scripture as appearing as a cherub, a serpent, a dragon, and even an angel of light, yet he remains Satan. Angels of God have also appeared in various forms, whether as radiant beings, ordinary men, or fierce warriors, depending on their assignment. In my case, it was a demonic manifestation. If I had not done preemptive work in prayer, the strength of that manifestation would have led me straight into a minefield of spiritual warfare once I arrived in England. I had something in common with the very enemy I needed to subdue, and that spiritual enemy would have used that unresolved agreement to harm me and possibly my family too.

We can't overlook these spiritual dynamics, which could turn into life and death in some situations. You simply can't overcome a demon with whom you have an agreement. The good news is that I didn't experience any significant warfare while in England, and while I was ministering at one church, a young woman bound to her wheelchair was supernaturally healed.

Who Are the Druids?

Druids come from the British Isles and areas of Western Europe, and most likely began in what is now modern Wales sometime before the fourth century BCE. Some classical writers even say that druidry dates back to the sixth century BCE, but we can't know for sure due to our lack of knowledge about the Druids.

> Druid beliefs are difficult to pin down since there are few records of their personal beliefs, philosophies, and practices. What is known about them comes from second (or even third) hand accounts from the Romans and the Greeks. . . . The druids outlawed written accounts of their practices. They strictly adhered to oral traditions, though they did have extensive knowledge of the written language and were all literate. They simply didn't want their sacred beliefs to fall into the wrong hands, which means that we have no reliable account detailing druidic practice.[2]

History tells us that the Druids were seen as seers, prophets, healers, magicians, and diviners—the assorted medicine men and witch doctors of the ancient world. Some of their rituals observed and recorded by others involved channeling gods and goddesses, and macabre forms of human sacrifice.[3]

When I've led people through a prayer of repentance and renunciation for bloodline druidism, those affected have exhibited unusually strong demonic manifestations. Like myself, they can never identify who practiced druidism in their bloodline, and they are usually caught off guard by the undeniable spiritual reflex. (In appendix A, I've written more about the Druids and their practices, and I've included some renunciation prayers for your consideration.)

This discourse might be shocking and even upsetting to some who can't believe that a Christian could exhibit an adverse spiritual reaction when the Holy Spirit uncovers a hidden familial connection with the occult. The reason it happens is that occult affiliations and practices are strongly binding within families and for generations after they first begin, because of their profoundly covenantal nature.

The Occult Grips Families Until Deliverance

To comprehend the workings of occult claims and bindings, it's essential to grasp what they mimic. They follow the profound metaphor of marriage deeply ingrained in Israelite culture. Here, God portrayed Himself as a nurturing and promise-keeping Husband to the entire nation of Israel and its descendants, visiting His promises upon them from generation to generation, even today. When the nation routinely committed idolatry with other gods and demons, He accused Israel of spiritual "prostitution" and "adultery," even giving her a "certificate of divorce" because Israel did not keep her covenant with Yahweh.[4] This brought wrath, punishment, curses, and long periods of captivity upon Israel and her future generations. Despite this, God pledged to reconcile with Israel and her descendants because they belonged to Him. He was not going to let go.

This marriage metaphor, a spiritually binding truth, is eerily mirrored by occult practices where demons, through human agents, seek dominion through binding covenants. Such agreements imply ownership not only of the individual but also of his or her offspring for generations. Demons may legally act on these agreements generation after generation, until they are severed through deliverance ministry. Deliverance ministry engages a spiritual "divorce" between demons and individuals and their families who have become unknowingly entangled through familial occult engagements. It offers a pathway to cutting these spiritual ties once and for all.

Defying or departing from these demonic covenants may lead to coercion or future attempts by these spirits or their proxies to reclaim individuals and their descendants. These spirits believe they have a legal right to the entire family. They do not let go easily and typically attempt to reenter the bloodline every successive generation. Thus, deliverance ministry is crucial for breaking free for both you and your family, and for those coming after you.

Most people have some form of occultism in their family line, or they have participated in aspects of the occult themselves. With that in mind, I encourage you to pray this prayer out loud to renounce the occult:

> In the name of Jesus, I repent of any and all occult rituals made by my forefathers and mothers or me. I renounce all dedications made by my ancestors or me to cults, cult leaders, and their demons. I break all ungodly and binding covenants associated with cults and occult practices, both to demons and to human beings. I break every claim for my life or my family through demonic rituals, dedications, and ungodly covenants. I fully dedicate myself and my family to the Lordship of Jesus Christ. Holy Spirit, I now invite You to come and be the ruling Spirit over my life and my family, in Jesus' name.[5]

Familiar Spirits Will Stop the New

The latest area of deliverance the Holy Spirit was singling out to me was more challenging to distinguish. I can honestly say that I was dealing with it in different forms for a solid year before I finally asked Him in total frustration, *What is this thing I keep dealing with?*

He responded clearly, *You are dealing with familiar spirits.* When I asked Him what to do about it, He said just as clearly, *They are standing in the way of the new things I am doing. You need to decree that they be devoured by fire.*

What is a decree? A decree is a verbal command based on an explicit promise from God. Job wrote, "Thou shalt also decree a thing, and it shall be established unto thee: and the light shall shine upon thy ways" (Job 22:28 KJV).

Familiar spirits are highly detested enemies of the Holy Spirit. Notice that He didn't tell me to ignore them, or to bind them, which is one remedy prescribed in the Scriptures.[6] He said to decree that they be devoured by fire. The nature of God's devouring fire is depicted in the psalms. King David wrote, "A fire goes before Him, and burns up His enemies round about" (Psalm 97:3). The fire of God will ignite His friends but consume His foes. Familiar spirits are coming under divine judgment, and it will be a great burning.

In her book *Breaking the Power of Familiar Spirits*, Kimberly Daniels gave this description of familiar spirits:

> A familiar spirit is any demonic assignment that surveys and studies people, territories, and bloodlines of families. The goal of their assignment is to gather spiritual intelligence that will open doors to instigate death and destruction. They enter and gain power in people's lives by disguising themselves as something common (familiar) while operating unawares through people, places, and things.[7]

One Bible dictionary says this about familiar spirits:

> The term is generally used to refer to the spirit of a dead person which professed mediums claimed they could summon for consultation (Deut. 18:11). The word "familiar" has in this phrase the sense of the Latin *familiaris*, belonging to one's family, and hence ready to serve one as a servant. Such a spirit was thought

to be able to reveal the future. They often resemble the family member in appearance (Isa. 8:19; 1 Sam. 28:7).[8]

There seem to be two primary manifestations of familiar spirits:

1. A familial demon or ancestral curse, as well as a spirit that becomes overly familiar with a person, place, or thing.
2. Witchcraft that employs divination, often channeled through mediums.

The Bible gives us clear instructions against any involvement with these spirits or those associated with them: "And when they say to you, 'Seek those who are mediums and wizards, who whisper and mutter,' should not a people seek their God? Should they seek the dead on behalf of the living?" (Isaiah 8:19). We see a poignant example in the story of King Saul that we find in 1 Samuel 28. Initially banning all mediums and spiritists from the land, Saul knew the danger of associating with them. Yet in a time of desperation before a battle with the Philistines, he sought out the medium of En Dor to summon the spirit of the prophet Samuel for counsel. There is scholarly debate over who or what appeared when the medium summoned Samuel. Some believe a familiar spirit appeared that resembled Samuel and accurately prophesied Saul's impending demise and Israel's defeat. Others believe it was actually Samuel's spirit that appeared.[9] Either way, this sobering tale is a powerful reminder of the consequences of seeking spiritual guidance outside of God's ordained ways.

"These evil spirits are called 'familiar' because they are attached to specific individuals, families, bloodlines, or places," wrote Kynan Bridges in his book *Overcoming Familiar Spirits*. He goes on, "A familiar spirit has an attachment to a particular area or areas of a person's life. They are acquainted with that person's mindsets and patterns of living."[10]

One minister tells a story about his visit to a medium who claimed to have communicated with his deceased father and grandfather. The medium shared things with the pastor that only he would have known. As a result, the pastor believed that he had resolved the unsettled issues from their lifetimes. As a result of his visit to the medium, he wrote in a post online, "I finally felt peace."

This pastor was in absolute deception. These were not the spirits of his grandfather and father speaking through the woman, but actual demons familiar with them. He mistook his feeling of peace as validation for his sin of consulting a medium, and he neglected a timeless truth from the Word of God. Associating with demons comes with consequences. He was now in spiritual debt to these demons, a debt to be collected not only in his lifetime but also in the lives of his offspring and their offspring too. He finished his post like this: "And I'm still preaching on Sunday," which was an indirect acknowledgment of wrongdoing by someone with no plan to repent.

Breaking the Cycle of Familiar Spirits

We empower familiar spirits through deeply ingrained personal beliefs that contradict God's Word—beliefs inherited from our families, reinforced by culture, and left unchecked for generations. These spirits often gain access through demonic covenants made in secrecy by past generations, and they continue to call out across time, afflicting today and tomorrow just as they did yesterday. Because these ingrained beliefs are so entrenched, breaking free from familiar spirits and the mindsets they fuel can feel like a lifelong battle. But with the power of Jesus, we don't just fight—we win.

Take the story of a woman who grew up under the influence of several generations of bitter, man-hating women. She was taught that men are untrustworthy, disposable, and only to be used for personal gain. That generational stronghold, amplified by the trauma of childhood molestation, culminated in a destructive rage so intense that she attempted to murder her second husband. Her first husband had already fled for his life. Prison became her turning point. It was there that she encountered the real Jesus—the Deliverer—and began dismantling the spiritual inheritance that had kept her family bound. What had been a curse of hatred became a testimony of redemption.

Generational cycles are real. They show up in chronic illnesses, marital breakdowns, financial struggles—patterns so persistent that they demand a deeper look. Just as doctors take a family medical history to identify genetic predispositions, we must recognize spiritual inheritances as well. I once knew a woman who was widowed in her early thirties, after her husband was killed. Years later, her daughter was also widowed in her early thirties. That's not a coincidence; that's a generational curse in action. Another man watched both his brothers die from disease and feared the same fate for himself. Without intervention, that pattern would come knocking at his door too. Just as medical intervention is necessary for physical conditions, spiritual intervention is crucial for breaking demonic cycles. You don't manage a curse; you break it.

Familiar spirits are bolder than ever. Occult activity is on the rise, spiritual boundaries have been weakened, and a culture obsessed with the supernatural has made room for these spirits to operate openly. Trauma, generational sin, and global spiritual warfare have all escalated their influence. But here's the good news: When the enemy comes in like a flood, the Spirit of the Lord raises a standard against him (see Isaiah 59:19). God is never caught off guard. He is always moving, always shaking, always setting His Church up for victory.

Malachi gives us a powerful promise: The spirit of Elijah is here to restore families (see Malachi 4:5–6). This is no small thing; it's a prophetic move of God! Throughout Scripture, genealogies serve as more than historical records; they're evidence of generational blessing and divine destiny. Just look at Matthew 1: "Abraham begot Isaac, Isaac begot Jacob. . . . Eliud begot Eleazar, Eleazar begot Matthan, and Matthan begot Jacob. And Jacob begot Joseph the husband of Mary, of whom was born Jesus who is called Christ" (verses 2, 15–16). These aren't just names; they're proof that God moves through generations to establish His purposes.

Now here's a game changer: If there are generational curses, it's because generational blessings came first. The enemy hijacks what God originally ordained for good. Those generational blessings may seem lost, but they are not gone forever. Familiar spirits are cunning; they disguise themselves as "just how our family is," making it difficult to recognize their grip. Many times, our usual spiritual warfare tactics don't seem to work against them. That's because these spirits are tied to strongholds, and strongholds require strategic dismantling. When we understand how these spiritual forces operate, which is what we'll look at in the next chapter, we can expose their schemes, tear down their influence, and step back into our rightful inheritance.

You are not destined to live under a curse. You are called to reclaim the blessings of your bloodline. It's time to break the cycle and take back what the enemy has stolen.

KINGDOM REFLECTIONS

1. Ancestral spirits, also known as *familiar spirits* or *family spirits*, are demons that attach themselves to families, often masquerading as deceased relatives.

2. When the Holy Spirit calls me to intercede for a nation, my focus is on dismantling the demonic strongholds that empower territorial spirits. Before I can move forward in prayer, I always examine my heart, ensuring that there are no personal connections or agreements with those spirits.

3. To grasp how occult practices operate and understand the demonic bondages they create, we need to understand how they counterfeit the biblical covenant of marriage.

4. Familiar spirits are among the most detestable enemies of the Holy Spirit. He didn't tell me to ignore them, or to bind them, which is one remedy prescribed in Scripture. He said to decree that they be devoured by fire.

5. Generational challenges such as chronic illness, marital discord, or financial struggles often plague our families across generations. Much as doctors inquire about a family's medical history, understanding generational curses is essential for identifying patterns that recur from generation to generation.

KINGDOM QUESTIONS

1. Do you come from a family that practices ancestral worship or has ties to occult traditions? If so, are you feeling any pressure to participate in these practices, and how are you navigating this spiritually?

2. Have you experienced personal deliverance from something that was rooted in the sins or iniquities of your ancestors? Was this a surprise to you, or did you expect that these generational issues might need to be confronted?

3. What's your perspective on the intense physical and emotional manifestations some people experience during deliverance? Is it always this dramatic, or are there other ways deliverance can take place that may be less visible but equally powerful?

4. Are familiar spirits hindering your progress? If so, what new spiritual or personal breakthrough do you sense they are trying to block, and how might you address this in prayer and action?

5. Have you observed destructive patterns repeating in your family line—whether in relationships, health, finances, or other areas? Could these patterns be indicative of a family curse or a generational stronghold that needs to be broken?

Understanding Strongmen and Strongholds

Just before the world flipped upside down with COVID, Tricia Turnbow was gearing up to conduct a series of prayer strikes in Europe—Estonia, London, France, and Italy. Tricia and her husband, Todd, copastor The Worship Center (TWC) in Lubbock, Texas. They began in 1997 with their first church plant there and have now expanded to three campuses. Tricia's trip to Europe culminated after years of prophetic dreams that led her to undertake prayer strikes in all these places. I will also add that the stories of her prayer assignments are totally wild and undeniably authored by the Holy Spirit.

Only days before Tricia left for Europe, she learned that a life-sized statue of Molech would be unveiled in the Colosseum of Rome at the precise time of her visit. You might remember reading about this ancient Canaanite deity in the Bible. This deity's name can be translated as "the personified ruler of shameful sacrifice." Molech was associated with some of the most horrific rituals imaginable. Molech worship wasn't just about illicit sexual rites; it involved the chilling practice of child sacrifice—what they called "passing children through the fire."[1]

Envision these enormous ancient statues, towering figures of a man with a bull's head. Each statue had a gaping hole in its belly, and possibly outstretched arms forming a ramp leading to this dreadful cavity. A fire blazed either inside or around these nightmarish idols. Infants were placed in the statue's arms or shoved into the hole. The grim belief was that by sacrificing their firstborn, families could secure Molech's favor, ensuring both their financial success and the prosperity of their future offspring.[2]

Tricia pressed on with the trip and carried out her prayer strikes in various cities, including Rome. The spiritual warfare in Rome suddenly escalated before she and her team confronted the unsettling appearance of Molech. Physical ailments struck hard at her prayer team—from digestive disorders to a sudden infection, and then one team member suddenly couldn't walk.

"We had a tough time locating the ginormous statue in the Colosseum, almost like it was behind a spiritual veil and hidden from us," Tricia pointed out. "Looking back, that was probably God's protection on us."

She admitted that she had been full of righteous anger and may have addressed the idol recklessly if they had found it sooner, thus causing a vicious spiritual backlash. After searching and searching, they located the statue's whereabouts outside the Colosseum and could only address it from behind a protective fence.

"We felt strongly to pray about the countless child sacrifices made to this deity," Tricia said. "We stood in repentance for every act and motive for sacrifice we could think of."

Feeling accomplished, Tricia and her prayer warriors left Rome just three days before the world went into lockdown.

She never expected that her battle on foreign ground for spiritual authority along this line would translate into spiritual authority in her own city. In 2021, a conversation began in Lubbock and gained traction through Project Destiny, a coalition of Kingdom-minded civic leaders and pro-life advocates. The conversation centered on the question, *Could Lubbock become a sanctuary city for the unborn?* This largely pro-life community rallied to get this initiative on the ballot, which involved holding town hall meetings, rallying community voices, and pressing the mayor and city council for support.

"I was shocked to see our conservative mayor and council fight against us as hard as they did," Tricia said.

Despite their resistance and some clear challenges posed by organizations like Planned Parenthood, the citizens of Lubbock, Texas, succeeded in bringing the issue to a citywide vote in May 2021, and it passed. Lubbock officially became the first and largest city with an actual Planned Parenthood provider to pass this revolutionary measure.

"The fruits of our labor in Lubbock were profound," Tricia reflected. "Abortion services ceased within the city, and then Governor Abbott declared the entire state a sanctuary for the unborn, with Lubbock as a pivotal hub."

The 350,000-strong university city became a beacon for other smaller towns to follow suit, creating a network of sanctuary cities across Texas. The initiative prevailed despite encountering resistance from some local officials and being met with threats, vandalism, and mischief. Tricia recognized the connection between her prayer strike and confrontation with Molech in Rome and its aftermath in Lubbock. It was a testament to the power of prayer and perseverance.

"We must have gained a real and genuine spiritual authority over Molech during this prayer assignment in Italy," she reflected. "An authority that threw down a spiritual Molech in our city and possibly our entire state." Tricia believed that the statue of Molech, which they had searched for in Rome but could barely see behind a protective fence, symbolized the barriers they faced and the divine protection and guidance that finally led them to victory. "The law stood firm in our city and state, and was further solidified by the overturning of Roe v. Wade," she said enthusiastically.

Both Rome and Lubbock demonstrate a spiritual principle we must learn about and understand. These destructive issues began with spiritual strongmen, or demons, and were carried out through strongholds, which are beliefs that empower strongmen. It is these strongholds that ultimately infect the family tree and empower the familiar.

Bind the Strongman

In the gospel of Mark, we encounter a powerful moment where Jesus confronts a severe accusation. Some Jewish scribes claimed He was casting out demons by the power of Beelzebub, another name for Satan. They insinuated that Jesus was merely a puppet of the prince of demons. Jesus countered their argument with a compelling parable: "If a kingdom is divided against itself, that kingdom cannot stand. And if a house is divided against itself, that house cannot stand. And if Satan has risen up against himself, and is divided, he cannot stand, but has an end" (Mark 3:24–26). He then explained that to plunder the strongman's house, one must first bind him. Jesus clearly identifies Satan as the "strongman" and portrays Himself as the victorious one coming to reclaim what belongs to God—our souls.

This parable holds profound relevance for us today. As followers of Christ, we are called to rise up and "bind the strongman" who seeks to exert control over our lives, churches, and regions. To *bind* means "to restrict, lock, tie-down, hold back, and keep [something] from doing what it wants to do."³ This is accomplished through our authoritative prayer and commands.

The nature of these commands will vary based on the strongman we confront, making it crucial to identify such spiritual forces and understand their influence.

To grasp the concept of strongmen, let's examine two biblical passages. In Ezekiel 28, God's message through the prophet Ezekiel appears to be directed at the human prince of Tyre. Yet beginning in verse 12, the language shifts, revealing a being with supernatural qualities—the anointed cherub who became profane with iniquity, an allusion to Lucifer. Similarly, Isaiah 14 starts with a judgment against the king of Babylon. It, too, transitions to address Lucifer, demonstrating a dual reference to both a human ruler and the spiritual entity exerting its influence.

A "strongman" represents a demon, while a "stronghold" is a mental fortress of lies built over time that provides access to and empowers these demons. There are strongmen who control nations, regions, and individuals through personal and cultural strongholds. Jesus encourages us that to "plunder his goods," we must first bind the strongman (Mark 3:27). Although the following list might vary somewhat from expert to expert, these are the strongmen in the Bible:

antichrist spirit	spirit of heaviness
spirit of bondage	spirit of infirmity
deaf and dumb spirit	spirit of jealousy
spirit of death	lying spirit
spirit of divination	perverse spirit
spirit of error	seducing spirit
familiar spirit	spirit of poverty
spirit of fear	spirit of whoredoms[4]
spirit of haughtiness	

Some spiritual strongmen, like the spirit of divination and a familiar spirit, don't operate alone; they form alliances to reinforce their influence. A familiar spirit in particular collaborates with each of these other strongmen, while some of them may also unite with each other to strengthen their hold. In some cases, these could be the same demonic entities operating through a family line, while in other cases, the spirits are entirely separate. Familiar spirits have a layered and deceptive nature, making their influence even more complex.

This strategy of demonic alliances isn't new. It reflects ancient military tactics such as we find in Genesis 14, where four kings joined forces against five, plundering cities and capturing Lot. But Abraham refused to accept defeat. He rose up, fought back, and rescued his nephew from captivity. In the same way, we are called to discern and dismantle the enemy's alliances through spiritual authority and strategic warfare.

My point is that countless individuals are held captive in various ways, some by multiple strongmen working together. This understanding shifts how we approach prayer. Like human generals commanding their armies, each demonic strongman leads a host of lesser spirits that oppress people, cities, and nations. Recognizing these dynamics can help us more skillfully empower our intercession and deliverance efforts. Jesus instructed us first to bind the strongman and then to plunder his house. Plundering involves expelling the army serving the strongman.

Take the strongman of fear, for instance. It has an entire roster of minions under its control—phobias, nightmares, heart-stopping terror, anxiety, stress, a crippling lack of trust, and more. The strongman of error leads a different cohort of spirits under its command—false doctrines, unteachability, rebellion, corruption, and others. Similarly, the deaf and dumb spirit governs a distinct team, encompassing afflictions such as muteness, hearing loss, emotional distress, drowning sensations, mental illness, blindness, seizures, and various other impairments. Such spirits are relentlessly dedicated to fortifying their strongholds in your life.[5]

This kind of discussion leaves us with some essential questions about our individual spiritual autonomy: *How, then, do we explain spiritual manifestations that can and do appear demonic? Is it possible for a Christian to be demon-possessed and in need of deliverance?*

Can a Christian Be Possessed?

As a new Christian, I experienced a profound deliverance from some spiritual bondage of my occult past. During a house prayer meeting, a discerning woman identified a spirit of sorcery over me. At that moment of revelation, I was violently thrown against the wall by an unseen entity and caught in a dramatic demonic manifestation that shook me to my core.

This event challenged the belief within my church that true Christians filled with the Holy Spirit couldn't manifest demons. Yes, I had the Holy Spirit, but those lingering areas of occult influence had to be confronted head on. Thankfully, I found my spiritual authority in Christ during that season and began my entrance into true freedom.

Since that powerful encounter, I've met countless Christians needing similar deliverance. For example, Kyra (not her real name) came forward for help after a church service. Though she was a devoted Christian and baptized in the Holy Spirit, she was suddenly overtaken by a strong demonic manifestation. Like me, she needed to confront her violent upbringing in satanism and the occult. This illustrates a vital truth: Christians can be demonized due to unresolved issues from their past.

Let me emphasize this crucial point: It's a myth to believe that Christians cannot be demonized. Notice that I use the term *demonized*, not *possessed*. This distinction is where much of the confusion arises. Possession and demonization are not the same thing. The late Derek Prince passionately addressed this issue, stating that the term *demon-possessed* in specific biblical passages is often mistranslated. For instance, Mark 1:32 (NIV) says, "That evening after sunset the people brought to Jesus all the sick and demon-possessed." Prince clarified,

> The word *possessed* suggests ownership. If you're demon-possessed, then you're owned by a demon. Now, I don't believe that any born-again, sincere Christian can be owned by a demon. . . . But the Greek word that's used can easily be, and should be, translated *demonized*.[6]

He went on to explain that even born-again Christians can experience demonization. There are areas of their personality where the Holy Spirit is not in complete control because there's a demon that needs to be addressed.

The question remains, then, *How much of a Christian can a demon possibly demonize?* In examining this, we must recognize that we are all made up of three parts: spirit, soul, and body. When Jesus comes into your life, He enters your spirit and takes up residence. Paul wrote to the Galatians, "I have been crucified with Christ and I no longer live, but Christ lives in me" (Galatians 2:20 NIV). I believe Charles H. Kraft, founder of Deep Healing Ministries, says it best: "A demon cannot live in a Christian's spirit—that is, the person's central core, the part that died when Adam sinned, because Jesus now lives there."[7]

All of this necessitates even further discussion of the deep need for inner healing and deliverance ministry churchwide, which is another controversial topic within Christianity.

The Power of Inner Healing and Deliverance

A respected church leader, Jeff, was known for his wisdom and calming presence in his ministry and among church members. Beneath this composed exterior, however, he faced a significant struggle at home. Despite his serene public demeanor, Jeff often lost his temper over minor issues, reacting with unexpected intensity. His wife had subtly distanced herself emotionally to avoid conflict, and their children were frequently on the receiving end of his harsh words. Although Jeff was not physically abusive, his verbal outbursts had a profound impact on his family, leaving deep emotional wounds. This disconnect between his public and private selves pointed to deeper issues. His outbursts were driven by a sense of losing control, with the strongman of fear dominating his life. But beneath that, there were deep-rooted strongholds—emotional scars from a childhood shaped by trauma and abuse. Jeff's healing journey required inner healing and deliverance ministry to confront a myriad of emotional triggers and work through layers of unforgiveness before the strongman of fear lost access to his life.

Deliverance ministry is a powerful and life-changing experience that brings freedom and transformation. Whether you are stepping into self-deliverance or working with a trusted inner healing and deliverance minister, the goal is the same—lasting freedom in Christ. Self-deliverance happens when a Christian, using his or her God-given authority in Jesus' name, partners with the Holy Spirit to repent, and to renounce every unclean spirit and command it to leave. Self-deliverance is a way to walk in daily freedom, even without a minister present. If you face something you cannot manage with self-deliverance, however, then it's time to engage a trusted minister and get the additional help you need.[8] At its core, deliverance ministry reveals where the enemy has gained access through lies and strongholds. It is a journey of identifying the sins, deceptions, and generational patterns that have opened the door to the enemy, and then closing that door for good.

True freedom comes through repentance—a deep, heartfelt turning to God as you acknowledge your sins and wrong choices. Repentance is a spiritual act of war that slams shut every open door to the enemy, reclaiming the legal authority over your soul. Once you've repented, you can rise up boldly and command the strongman and every demonic spirit connected to him to leave, knowing they have no right to stay.

From my observations and personal experiences with inner healing and deliverance, I have found that they are most effective when intertwined rather than approached separately. I wrote about this extensively in my *Inner Healing and Deliverance Handbook*. Remember, the apostle Peter described Jesus as anointed with the Holy Spirit's power to heal all who were oppressed by the devil (see Acts 10:38). This Scripture beautifully links healing and deliverance, showing us that they are intricately connected in God's redemptive work.

That's why inner healing and deliverance ministry is absolutely crucial. It's not just about casting out demons; it's about dismantling deep-seated strongholds—especially those generationally entrenched belief systems that empower these spirits. When you take down the strongman, you're left facing the stronghold itself. As Paul reminds us, "For though we walk in the flesh, we do not war according to the flesh. For the weapons of our warfare are not carnal but mighty in God for pulling down strongholds" (2 Corinthians 10:3–4). Bringing down these strongholds isn't a quick fix, however. It demands time, spiritual resilience, and unwavering determination.

Strongholds Take Time to Dismantle

Marcus was in the thick of marital turmoil. What started as minor disagreements escalated into fiery confrontations, revealing an unsettling truth: His wife's rage often took on a strength that defied her physical frame. In the heat of her rage, she would lash out physically and brand him as weak while verbally attacking his male identity.

As they began to navigate the storm of their emotional upheaval, Marcus also decided to confront his past honestly. Before surrendering to Christ, he had dabbled in a short-lived homosexual relationship in college—a chapter that nearly derailed his life. "I was engulfed in confusion and felt an overwhelming pull toward that world," he shared. "It took everything I had to reclaim my identity and purity after that experience."

In hindsight, he recognized this struggle as a spiritual battle, a clash with the strongman of perversion. He thought his battle was contained, until he witnessed his wife enter a nearly possessed state and target the very identity he had fought so hard to protect. It became clear that this familiar demon had returned but was manifesting in a new way.

Together, Marcus and his wife faced their deep emotional strongholds, working diligently to close the door to the strongman of perversion. Their journey wasn't just about confronting the demon; it was about transforming their thought patterns and belief systems that empowered the strongman. Marcus realized that his open door stemmed from a deep father wound, linking him to a familiar spirit rooted in family trauma. Healing and changing his beliefs took a long time. He had moments, even days, when he wondered if he was making progress at all.

When troubling thoughts or behaviors linger after personal deliverance, remember that it usually doesn't mean the demon is still present. Instead, it signals that mental strongholds still need dismantling. You might feel powerless to change initially, but you are not. With perseverance and spiritual authority in Christ, you can break down these barriers and fully embrace the freedom that deliverance promises.

Do you know how to begin? Start by diving deep into God's truth through His Word. Meditate on it and declare it over your life. If thoughts of fear are your stronghold, start with this powerful Scripture: "For God has not given us a spirit of fear, but of power and of love and of a sound mind" (2 Timothy 1:7). If perversion dominates your thoughts, read through Romans chapter 6, and then commit verse 14 to memory, personalizing it: "Sin does not have dominion over me." In the areas where I've dealt with strongholds in me, I've proclaimed key Scriptures over myself countless times to dismantle those deeply rooted beliefs. Remember, God's Word is a hammer and a sword. It slices through generational lies and shatters internal barriers. When you keep pressing in with faith and perseverance, those strongholds will eventually fall.

From the Personal to the Territorial

Like Tricia Turnbow, I am also led by the Holy Spirit to pray in different places worldwide. In like manner, I have often emerged with mighty spiritual authority that I wouldn't have attained any other way. In my book *Glory Carriers*, I wrote how I had led three intercessory trips into China and was praying about a fourth one. While praying, I heard the Holy Spirit speak with unusual clarity: *Don't go to China. Go to Thailand and intercede there.*

I obeyed His directive, but we did not accomplish the entire prayer assignment on that trip. We prayed in some key areas, but I felt as if there was more to accomplish. We were back in Thailand the following year, guided by a seasoned apostle in Bangkok and his dedicated team. They pointed us toward Chiang Mai, where this apostle was establishing a new church. Eager to support the mission, we ventured to this northern city and were led by the Holy Spirit to complete our prayer assignment in a colossal Buddhist temple perched high on a mountain.

The temple was an awe-inspiring fortress, dominating the landscape from its lofty perch. As we stood there, I couldn't shake the image of the Bible's many accounts of false worship at high places—those ancient, pagan altars set atop hills or beneath grand trees, intended to draw people closer to their false gods. These high places were not just relics of the past; they were a blatant affront to God, both then and now. I was also shocked to hear from this apostle and his team that most of the profoundly perverse sins that we've come to associate with Thailand had their beginnings in this temple. I have not been able to verify this in my internet research, but I'll take their word for it.

Our mission was evident as we wandered through the temple grounds. We sought repentance for Thailand's sins and prayed fervently to dismantle strongholds. We zeroed in on the strongmen of religion and perversion, determined to break their hold. I can still hear the echo of those Buddhist monks ringing their bells, a constant and rhythmic call to prayer that has been part of their practice for centuries. Those bells, clanging persistently, seemed to punctuate our prayers, reminding us of the spiritual intensity of the place.

After hours of intercession, we felt a deep sense of accomplishment. We descended the most colossal outdoor staircase I've ever seen, so wide it felt like a grand avenue. We formed a circle at the base of these expansive stairs and exuberantly thanked God for the day. At that moment, heaven felt as though it had opened, and the presence of the Holy Spirit descended upon us like a tangible wave. It was a scene reminiscent of Luke 3:21–22, where Jesus was baptized and prayed, and the heavens opened, with the Holy Spirit descending like a dove. Our experience mirrored that divine response, and we couldn't contain our joy, erupting in loud claps, shouts, and praises to Jesus. The intensity of the moment was overwhelming—so much so that in hindsight, I realized we might have tipped the surrounding Buddhist worshipers into a small riot. But honestly, I wouldn't trade that experience for anything.

After leaving Thailand, and in profound contrast, we flew to Norway on our way to a conference in Sweden. As we crossed the Swedish border, I suddenly and distinctly sensed the presence of two formidable strongmen. I dubbed them Thor and Frigg, partly in jest, but these principalities seemed to hold sway over the cultural strongholds and practices of the region. Being half Swedish, I've always been unusually attuned to the spiritual climate there. Even so, I knew I wasn't called to confront these entities directly. Jesus, our great High Priest and Chief Intercessor, hadn't given me that assignment. Looking back, I believe this was a protective boundary God set in place to shield me from any ancestral spirits that could have affected me. I've had many spiritual experiences in Sweden that indicate there might be areas of my life that still need spiritual deliverance from the familiar, and I trust that this will happen in His timing.

Since we were not on assignment to tear the strongmen down in Sweden, we prayed a simple prayer to bind these spirits from interfering with our mission, ensuring that our ministry could proceed without hindrance. Again, to bind something, we wield our words with authority. We proclaimed, "We bind these ruling spirits in the name of Jesus. We prohibit them from working against us in any capacity. Our mission here in Sweden will proceed without demonic disruption, in Jesus' name." Our approach worked. The conference was a resounding success and was filled with powerful ministry.

Remember that strongmen can control entire regions and communities through powerful mental strongholds. This is why certain places and cultures resonate with specific identities. Look at Las Vegas, famously known as "Sin City." Behind that label, powerful strongmen are at work, all supported by a network of regional strongholds that give them access.

Similarly, the Middle East is often recognized for its association with Islam, including some of its more extreme and violent expressions. I believe a strongman is at play here—the "prince of Persia," the territorial demon we read about in the book of Daniel. This prince has been fortified over generations by the belief systems and mental fortresses that have taken root and been passed down from generation to generation, becoming a familiar spirit that feels insurmountable.

Although they can be downright daunting, God has been speaking to me about these deeply entrenched strongholds. I want to challenge your perspective and prophesy that you will break through in this generation. You will find out why in the next chapter.

KINGDOM REFLECTIONS

1. A *strongman* refers to a demon, while a *stronghold* is a mental fortress built from lies over time.

2. Strongmen work to control individuals, regions, and even entire nations through both personal and cultural strongholds. This explains why certain geographical areas or cultural identities become known for specific strongholds—like Las Vegas, often called "Sin City."

3. Jesus made it clear that to "plunder the strongman's goods," we must first *bind* him (see Mark 3:27). To *bind* means to restrict, lock up, tie down, and prevent a spiritual strongman from carrying out its agenda.

4. Just as a general leads an army, each demonic strongman commands a host of lesser spirits that work to oppress individuals, cities, and nations.

5. Inner healing and deliverance ministry are essential in confronting strongmen and dismantling their strongholds. Casting out demons is not enough; we must also dismantle the deep-seated, generational belief systems and mindsets that have empowered these spirits.

KINGDOM QUESTIONS

1. Have you ever experienced what could be described as demonization? How did you recognize the signs, and how did you respond?

2. What does true repentance look like? Why is repentance such a powerful key in unlocking inner healing and deliverance—both for you personally and for those you minister to?

3. After reading this chapter, do you recognize any specific beliefs or mindsets in your life or family that might be reinforcing strongholds? How might these beliefs be empowering spiritual strongmen?

4. Are there dominant cultural or spiritual strongholds in your region or nation? How do these broader influences affect you, your community, or the spiritual climate around you?

5. Are you called to intercession? How can you apply the truths from this chapter in your prayer assignments to confront and dismantle spiritual strongholds on behalf of others?

You'll Break Through in This Generation

In a spiritually electrified part of the world, where ancestral traditions ran deep and legacy carried weight like a heavy yoke, Abeiku's father made what seemed like an honorable pact with his trusted friend. What looked like a simple act of loyalty—wrapped in cultural devotion and tradition—triggered a chain reaction they never saw coming. It was the kind of decision that would shake their bloodlines to the core.

"This man was first my friend, and then he became my father's closest companion," Abeiku recalls. "He had a way about him—always upbeat, always hopeful, and deeply tied to the rich heritage of the Akan Ashanti people."

Like so many in that culture, having a son to carry on his name wasn't just this friend's dream—it was nonnegotiable. Legacy was everything.

Yet a painful reality loomed over the man. His wife wasn't conceiving, and with every passing year, the unspoken weight of infertility became unbearable. You could almost feel the tension clawing at their marriage. Frustrated, he finally confided in Abeiku's father, saying, "My wife needs to get it together." As if the burden of barrenness rested solely on her shoulders.

That's when Abeiku's father—deeply rooted in the spiritual customs of their people—offered a solution. A spiritual transaction. A ritual. A high-stakes covenant performed by a powerful witch doctor. This wasn't just some simple prayer request. No, this was an invitation into the unseen realm, a pact with forces that don't give without taking.

Desperate, this friend agreed. The ritual was performed, and like clockwork, his wife conceived. A daughter was born.

Almost immediately, things began to shift for this family. Doors flung open—promotions, favor, a radical transformation in their circumstances. Before long, they moved to the United States, stepping into a new life packed with unexpected opportunities. It was clear something was working behind the scenes, orchestrating their success.

Spiritual agreements, however, are never without consequence.

For years before their move, this family had made monthly pilgrimages to a mountain shrine in Ghana, a sacred place where they honored the spiritual forces they believed had given them their child. They had sacrificed. They had worshiped. And with each visit, they had reaffirmed their commitment to the pact.

Then they moved to America, and the rituals stopped. Distance from their homeland weakened their spiritual obligations, and the consequences of neglect came swiftly. In the early 1990s, Abeiku's father visited these friends in New York. Almost immediately, he fell gravely ill and landed in the hospital.

"It was as if the pact had begun to unravel," Abeiku says. "And the thought of my father dying on foreign soil was unthinkable."

Though Abeiku's father recovered enough to return from New York to Ghana, something had shifted. His body broke down—diabetes, high blood pressure, sickness upon sickness. The once-vibrant man withered under the weight of an unseen burden.

"That trip to New York was the turning point," Abeiku reflects. "It set something in motion that couldn't be undone."

A few years later, his father died.

Then came an eerie twist. His father's friend passed away within days. Two men, bound by blood and by spirit, sealed by a covenant they didn't fully understand, went to the grave almost simultaneously. In keeping with Ghanaian tradition, their bodies had to be transported back to their ancestral home. This was the neighborhood where they had once lived side by side. Their hearses passed through the same streets on the same day. Both were buried that day.

The repercussions did not stop there. Years later, Abeiku found out that the friend's wife had also died, which meant their daughter was likely left orphaned in New York. The chilling part is that this daughter has no idea that she is still tied to a spiritual contract, because Abeiku has not been able to locate her.

"This isn't just my family's story," Abeiku says. "This is a warning. Spiritual agreements don't just disappear because we ignore them. Every decision we make—especially in the supernatural—has weight. It shapes our destiny. And sometimes, it shackles the generations after us in chains that must be broken."

Deliverance is real, but so are the consequences of spiritual ignorance. Some doors were never meant to be opened. And when they are, they don't close without a fight.

Hope to Heal Ancestral Chains

Have you ever considered the recurring patterns of tragedy that seem to haunt your family tree? Manifestations of addiction, early death, infertility, madness, perversion, rejection, and more—harsh realities that God never intended, yet that often cling to us across generations. Tragically, many people mistake the enemy's schemes for God's will, leaving these destructive forces unchallenged and unchecked.

If you're unsure of the source of these struggles, dive into the truth of John 10:10. Here, Jesus unveils the thief—Satan—who comes "to steal, and to kill, and to destroy." In striking contrast, Jesus proclaims, "I have come that they may have life, and that they may have it more abundantly." The Greek word for abundant, *perissos*, means "exceedingly, very highly, beyond measure, more, superfluous."[1] This promise of abundance bursts with hope and expectancy, starkly contrasting the heartache many have experienced in their family histories.

Consider the Israelites, whom God commanded to drive out every Canaanite tribe from their Promised Land. The Hebrew Bible regarded the Canaanites and their associated groups, which were the Amorites, Girgashites, Hittites, Hivites, Jebusites, and Perizzites, as making up what tradition calls the "seven nations of Canaan." These people groups were to be resisted or actually destroyed by the Israelites.[2] This divine directive was more than a military conquest; it was a protective measure against the horrific worship practices of the Canaanites, and against the Israelites' tendency to intermarry and adopt the idolatry themselves. Remarkably, it took several centuries for the Israelites to fulfill this command, with the Jebusites proving particularly tenacious.

This powerful narrative mirrors the journeys of countless families, including many Christians. We've been entrusted with the divine charge to break these generational chains, yet we often watch our loved ones remain trapped by the same historically destructive patterns. If this strikes a chord with you, take heart. I believe that what you have grieved over for generations will be transformed in this generation. A breakthrough of healing and restoration is being unleashed to transform your family legacy.

The Weight of Unresolved Issues

Do you dream at night? I often do, with my dreams being brief yet rich in meaning. While writing this book, I had two back-to-back dreams about my late grandmother from my biological father's side. When a subject appears multiple times in one night, it's a signal to pay attention—God is speaking. Writing these dreams down and turning them into prayer points is crucial.

In the first dream, my grandmother was deceased but had left behind a single white suitcase filled with items. The dream revealed her frugal yet messy nature and that she had never unpacked her belongings. She was also deceased in the second dream, which featured a tall, white kitchen sink, one she had struggled to use due to her short stature. As a result, she had not washed her dishes properly and had left many things unclean.

A bit of background: In the 1920s, my grandmother attended Gustavus College in Minnesota, where she fell in love with her professor. They married, and she became an elementary school teacher. They also raised five boys together. My grandparents were typical Scandinavians—reserved, conservative, and dry-humored, yet good-natured. Despite their conservative parenting and influence, something terribly dark corrupted my biological father, leading him down a path of profound evil.

My dreams of my paternal grandmother revealed that she could not unpack or address her own issues. I then wondered what life event had haunted her. Did she experience childhood trauma? A brush with the occult? Was there a history of rejection? I've learned the hard way that whatever you don't deal with will eventually deal with you. It will show up in your children too. Her hidden and unfinished narrative unfolded in her five sons, revealing a heartbreaking family curse. Consider that well before she had reached the century mark, she lost three sons to early deaths—two of whom battled alcoholism and schizophrenia, while the third, a devoted family man, tragically perished in a car accident in his thirties. The remaining two were both medical professionals and led relatively stable lives, although one faced divorce and remarriage, and the other never married. They both lived into their eighties.

Through these dreams, I began to see my grandmother in a new light. I never perceived her as troubled, yet the struggles of her sons spoke volumes. Something had been opened in her that needed to be closed—a generational curse still affecting her grandchildren and great-grandchildren today. Regardless, I am determined to break this cycle of iniquity. I am the generation that overcomes it.

The Mystery of Iniquity

Iniquity—what a powerful word! It means to bend or distort the heart, pointing to a specific weakness or tendency toward sin. Isaiah boldly declares that Christ was "bruised for our iniquities" (Isaiah 53:5), and let me tell you, that's not just a nice thought; it's a life-altering truth.

Here's the reality: If you sin once, repent, and genuinely move on, that's the end of it. But when you keep sinning the same way over and over again, it transforms from sin into iniquity—a vicious cycle that takes root and begins to define you. It becomes your "bent," and given the right circumstances, it just spills out of you.

This isn't just personal; it's generational. When a sin is practiced repeatedly, it becomes iniquity and passes down through the bloodline to the children. Each generation, having a "bent" or tendency toward a particular sin, adds to this legacy of iniquity, making it harder and harder to resist the same sins.

Exodus 20:5 warns us about the iniquities of our forefathers: "You shall not bow down to them nor serve them. For I, the

LORD your God, am a jealous God, visiting the iniquity of the fathers upon the children to the third and fourth generations of those who hate Me." If we don't confront and cleanse these deep-seated issues, we risk watching our children mirror our mistakes, trapped in a cycle that feels impossible to break.

Look at author and minister Marilyn Hickey's testimony. Her family had a history of mental health struggles. Her father had two nervous breakdowns, and her great-grandfather was emotionally and mentally unwell. When she was thirty-six and under immense pressure, the enemy taunted her, saying, *You're just like your father. You'll break down like he did.*

She agreed with this deception, telling herself, *I am like my father, and I'll break down too.*

But God broke through that lie, reminding her, *You're like your true Father. I've never had a nervous breakdown, and neither will you!*

She had a complete turnaround in response to His words.[3]

Jesus was bruised for our iniquities. His wounds on the cross aren't just for show; they provide the ultimate restoration. We can break free from our bents toward iniquity and reclaim our God-given design. Marilyn Hickey offered this illustration:

> The difference between a wound and a bruise is that if you wound yourself, it will eventually scab over and heal. A bruise, however, can stay around for a long time. It may become discolored and can even go so deep as to bruise the bone. An iniquity can be compared to a bruise because it stays around and goes to the bone from generation . . . to generation . . . to generation.[4]

Paul calls this the "mystery of iniquity" in 2 Thessalonians 2:7 (KJV). It's the hidden link between a parent's sins and the children's paths. If a parent is a liar or a thief, his or her children often follow the same patterns.

Two Christian friends were churchgoing, worshipful, and active in Christian ministry, but both had a distinct bent of family iniquity. That bent was to chase money at any cost, and their family histories were notorious for this. Looking back, I had my doubts that the Holy Spirit birthed their friendship, even though they both said they were Christians. Given that they had similar tendencies and family issues, it's more likely they had come together over what was familiar, an indicator that familiar spirits were involved. Was I surprised to hear that they collaborated over a money scheme that ultimately cost them their reputation, long-term friendships, and employment? No. What appeared to be subdued in their Christian walk was only dormant and waiting for an opportune time. Sadly, iniquity won again.

This true story should be a call to wake up, recognize these cycles, and confront them relentlessly and fervently. There are seasons when we need to examine our relationships and ask ourselves what brought us together. Is that relationship bringing you closer to God or closer to compromise? You might need to do some relational rearranging to reclaim your family legacy from the wiles of familiar spirits and reroute your family line toward the plans of the Holy Spirit.

The Roots of Iniquity

When God called His people out of Egypt and into the land of their forefathers, He gave them a shocking command—wipe out the seven Canaanite clans living there (see Deuteronomy 7:1–2; 20:16–18). Now, that might sound harsh to modern ears, but hold on. Once you see the full picture, you'll understand why this had to happen.

These seven tribes were all descendants of Canaan, the son of Ham and grandson of Noah—hence the name "Canaanites." But their story isn't just a history lesson; it's a sobering look at generational iniquity and how unchecked sin can spiral into full-blown wickedness.

Let's rewind to Noah. Scripture describes him as "perfect in his generations" and as one who "walked with God" (Genesis 6:9). Yet even this righteous man had some serious family drama. His son Ham opened the door to a generational curse through a moment of dishonor and sin. Genesis 9:21–22 records the pivotal event: "Then he [Noah] drank of the wine and was drunk, and became uncovered in his tent. And Ham, the father of Canaan, saw the nakedness of his father, and told his two brothers outside."

That word *uncovered* is no small thing. In Leviticus, it's consistently linked to serious sexual sins, usually involving incest. We read that when Noah sobered up, he made some inquiries and "found out what his youngest son had done to him" (Genesis 9:24 NIV). The wording suggests that Ham did more than just view his father's nakedness. Scholars debate exactly what went down in that tent, but one thing is clear—this was no innocent glance. The severity of Noah's reaction tells us that something far worse occurred. Some believe that Ham violated his own father in a predatory act, while others suggest that he slept with Noah's wife, making Canaan the by-product of that sin. Either way, what happened was vile enough for Noah to wake up, realize what had been done to him, and unleash a generational curse: "Cursed be Canaan; a servant of servants he shall be to his brethren" (verse 25).[5]

That curse didn't just stick—it spread. Ham's descendants carried this iniquity forward, especially the Amorites, one of the Canaanite tribes. These people weren't just casually sinful; they were utterly depraved. Their society was steeped in idol worship, sexual perversion, and blood rituals. Their religious practices included grotesque orgies and the veneration of false gods through acts so dark and twisted that God Himself declared their time was up.

We cannot ignore the profound weight of God's judgment on sin, particularly immorality. Scripture clearly reveals His deep displeasure with sexual sin, and the consequences are grave. I'm not sure of the origin, but we have a saying in our house: *What walks in the fathers will run in their sons.* This saying reflects the nature of iniquity. It tends to escalate through subsequent generations.

Corrupted Bloodlines Were Destroyed

In Genesis 15, God reassures Abram that he will inherit the Promised Land, explaining that his descendants would dwell in a foreign land for four hundred years. However, they would return after four generations because "the iniquity of the Amorites is not yet full" (Genesis 15:16 KJV).

Recall that in Genesis 13, Abram and his nephew Lot separated, with Lot choosing to settle near the cities of Sodom and Gomorrah, which the Canaanites inhabited. These cities were notorious for their sinful practices, including homosexuality, and they ultimately faced destruction as a result. Despite Abram's pleas for mercy, only the righteous Lot and his family were spared, as the rest of the inhabitants were utterly corrupt.

The "mystery of iniquity" had already manifested in Sodom and Gomorrah; the fathers' sins had permeated through the generations, reaching the third and fourth generation. After four generations of escalating iniquity, the children had become so twisted that they could not walk uprightly before the Lord. Their spiritual bloodline was thoroughly defiled, with their hearts inclined solely toward evil. Much like humanity before the Flood, these descendants had become corrupted beyond remedy.

It is sobering, but true. These bloodlines were too far gone, and judgment was the only option. But that was before the cross. Now we have what they did not. We have Jesus. What destroyed them does not have to destroy you. Jesus' blood breaks every curse and severs every iniquity.

At that time, God made it clear to Israel that this level of corruption could not be ignored or negotiated with. The iniquity in the land was so severe, so generationally entrenched, that the only solution was complete removal. So God commanded the Israelites,

> But of the cities of these peoples which the LORD your God gives you as an inheritance, you shall let nothing that breathes remain alive, but you shall utterly destroy them: the Hittite and the Amorite and the Canaanite and the Perizzite and the Hivite and the Jebusite, just as the LORD your God has commanded you.
>
> Deuteronomy 20:16–17

When Israel disregarded God's judgments, her people faced severe consequences. Remember that God's purpose was to preserve Israel's bloodline from also corrupting beyond repair. During the conquest of Canaan, God intervened in extraordinary ways, even causing the sun to stand still in a pivotal battle until Joshua emerged victorious (see Joshua 10:12–14). While the Israelites largely succeeded in defeating or driving out the Canaanites, they ultimately fell short of complete obedience. Some Canaanites were left to govern themselves, and in some instances, the Israelites even enslaved them instead of fully following God's command to eliminate them.

The promise of land was contingent upon the Israelites' adherence to God's commandments and their exclusive worship of Yahweh. Unfortunately, Israel could never remain faithful. God will not remove what you choose to tolerate, so the Canaanites were allowed to continue occupying the Promised Land and ensnaring Israel in their ways. But here's the good news: God never revokes His promises. Among the Canaanite tribes, the Jebusites stood out for their remarkable resilience. Though under God's judgment, they remained fortified in their stronghold for centuries, until King David arrived in power and the tides began to turn. This reminds us that generational promises are never abandoned, but an obedient generation will bring them to fruition. We can conquer what our forefathers could not overcome, and we will do it in this generation.

The Season of Fulfillment

The Israelites' struggle against the Jebusites illustrates a profound truth: The path to divine promise is often fraught with challenges and delays. Even though God commanded the Jebusites' destruction, it took centuries of conflict and perseverance for the Israelites to overcome this formidable tribe and fulfill His will. In the end, the Jebusites' legacy transformed into a pivotal chapter in the history of Jerusalem, a city destined to become central to the faith of millions.

In 2 Samuel 5:1–3, we see the tribes of Israel come to David at Hebron, recognizing his leadership. They declare, "Indeed we are your bone and your flesh" (verse 1). In a moment that had been years in the making, David, after a grueling decade of trials and tribulations, finally sees the realization of his anointing.

Picture it: David, once a fugitive running from the shadows of Saul, now stands at the threshold of his destiny. There's a lesson here for us—a stark reminder that fulfillment doesn't always come easy. For David, it was nearly ten years from Samuel anointing him to his rise as king—eight years of waiting, hiding, and fighting for what was promised. But then it happened. The promise was fulfilled, and the heavens echoed with the sound of destiny being unlocked.

The Fight for Promises

Make no mistake—God's promises are never handed to us without a fight. David's journey was not a walk in the park, but a battleground. He wasn't merely anointed king; he also endured years of conflict and chaos before sitting upon the throne. For David and for us, the fight for the fulfillment of promises often reveals the true strength of our faith.

In 2 Samuel 5:2, God speaks to David, saying, "You shall shepherd My people Israel, and be ruler over Israel." But before that promise could be realized, David faced the formidable Jebusites—a seemingly insurmountable obstacle. They laughed in the face of his aspirations, saying, "You'll never get in here! Even the blind and lame could keep you out!" (2 Samuel 5:6 NLT). They thought his attempts would be thwarted, and that mere human limitations could stop him.

But here lies the winning key: *You need a word.* God's promises are not just inspirational; they're strategic. The Bible is filled with them, covering every situation you will ever face. When you are up against resistance, God will breathe life into a specific Scripture, highlighting it to silence your doubts and fuel your faith. That word becomes your blueprint and your battle cry. And once God has spoken, it doesn't matter who mocks you or doubts your breakthrough. You have all that you need. Keep moving forward.

Confronting the Jebusites

Imagine the scene—David and his men stand at the foot of Zion, a fortress taunting them with its seemingly impregnable walls. The Jebusites, entrenched in their stronghold, feel invincible. But David doesn't flinch. He declares, "Whoever climbs up by way of the water shaft and defeats the Jebusites . . . he shall be chief and captain" (2 Samuel 5:8).

Here was David's revelation: The path to victory would not be through brute force alone, but through ingenuity and reliance on the Spirit of God. This water shaft challenge was akin to a triathlon, requiring a unique blend of skills: tunneling, climbing, and wielding a sword, all while leaning on divine strength for what seemed impossible.[6]

Joab, the fearless warrior, seized the opportunity, motivated by the promise of leadership. He was about to venture where no man had gone before, inspired by the glory of a conquest that would echo through generations. And when he conquered, we read the proud declaration, "Nevertheless David took the stronghold of Zion (that is, the City of David)" (2 Samuel 5:7). And that city is known as Jerusalem today. What took generations to conquer, David conquered in his generation.

A Generational Shift

And let me tell you, this is a pivotal moment for you too. You're standing at the edge of your own promises. You're in a time of generational breakthrough—what your forefathers could not conquer, you will conquer in this generation. This is your time to rise and take what has been promised, what has been long awaited.

As you stand firm, remember that you must keep what you've laid hold of. Like David, you will face challenges, naysayers, and perhaps even moments of doubt. But the promise is yours, and you must guard it fiercely. As you step forward into the fullness of what God has for you, you will find that He has equipped you with everything you need to overcome.

Are you ready for this moment? I believe you are. So let's discuss in the next chapter the distinct characteristics of those who move their families from the curse to the blessing. This is your fulfillment season, and you will step into your generational blessings.

KINGDOM REFLECTIONS

1. When we consider the command God gave to the Israelites to destroy the Canaanite tribes inhabiting the Promised Land, it can be shocking. Yet understanding the "mystery of iniquity" helps us grasp the gravity of God's directive (see 2 Thessalonians 2:7).

2. The command to wipe out the Canaanites was not merely a military conquest; it was a divine protection strategy. God's people were being safeguarded from the Canaanites' perverse worship practices and the dangerous temptation of intermarriage, which could lead Israel into idolatry and spiritual compromise.

3. Sin, when practiced repeatedly, morphs into iniquity—a deeply entrenched, generational bondage. Iniquity doesn't just stop with one generation; it gets passed down through the bloodline, with each new generation being even more predisposed to repeat the same sins.

4. Iniquity can intensify in successive generations over time. When Jesus is invited in, He breaks the cycle. He cuts through the pattern of iniquity and sets a new trajectory. What looks beyond repair is no match for His redemptive power.

5. God never forsakes His generational promises. It takes an obedient generation, however, to lay hold of and bring those promises to fruition.

KINGDOM QUESTIONS

1. The Israelites were commanded to *drive out* the Canaanites, yet many of these enemies were left in place, leading to Israel's bondage. Is there something you

have tolerated in your life that God has called you to *eliminate*?

2. Many people are living under spiritual agreements they never made themselves. Have you ever had dreams, visions, or strange encounters that might point to an unresolved spiritual debt?

3. What generational cycles in your family need to end *with you*? What would it look like for you to rise as the David of your bloodline and take down the Jebusite strongholds?

4. Iniquity is more than sin; it's a "bent," a pattern of dysfunction passed down through generations. What bents have you noticed in your family that need to be broken?

5. The enemy mocks those who try to break free, just as the Jebusites taunted David. What lies has the enemy whispered to you about your destiny? How can you use God's Word to silence them?

FOUR

When You're the First to Break Free

While attending to her two toddlers at the park, Olivia noticed an obese and yet sensually dressed Caucasian woman walking by. The woman reminded her of her mother's close relative, giving her a moment of pause. For no real reason, the woman spouted off to Olivia as she walked by, saying, "Don't forget where you came from."

Olivia then looked at her phone just in time to see my text and special request. As a pastor and prophetic minister, she recognized the sequence of events as a divine coincidence. She was being divinely summoned to present her testimony, and my text, which came in at the right moment, invited her to share her family story.

"My mother and father came together while my dad was married to somebody else," Olivia explained. "My mother moved in with him and forced his wife to move out." Her older brother was born before her mom and dad became legally married. Once they

71

were married, Olivia was conceived. Her father was a womanizer and an alcoholic. He frequented the bar next to their trailer home.

"My nickname is Moonlight Rose," Olivia explained. "It's the name of the bar where my dad was passed out on a pool table when my mom went into labor. He wouldn't wake up to take her to the hospital." Finally, completely drunk, he managed to wake up and take her. This nickname, reminiscent of that scene, deeply impacted Olivia for most of her life.

Olivia's mom and dad became homeless and lived in a tent outside her uncle's home. They fought constantly, and when Olivia was just a newborn, her father refused to let her mother back into the tent. Being extremely poor, her mom took the kids and left to find refuge with friends and relatives.

"We settled in at our maternal grandma's house when I was three or four years old, but my grandmother's boyfriend molested me," Olivia said. "When I told my mom, she grabbed me and took me outside to his work truck and then destroyed what she could of his truck in rage. We left that environment for a few years and then returned when it was safe."

Olivia's mom refused welfare and chose to work, meaning she wasn't home very much. When Olivia's older sister wasn't in juvenile hall, she became Olivia's caretaker.

"My brother was expelled from every school for fighting, and my sister was deep into gangs, just like her father," Olivia described. "She was my example. Like her, I lived to get high, drink, and be a fighter."

An intense atmosphere of fighting and violence filled their home. Often, there was physical fighting, especially between her mother and sister. Even in this environment, Olivia always believed in God's existence. In second grade, she went to a friend's church for a few months and wept at the altar after encountering the Holy Spirit. At parties during her teen years, she would preach to people while drunk, asking them why they didn't believe in God. She finally became a believer in Jesus at the age of eighteen, just after high school, and was radically changed.

"I was in a two-year relationship with my boyfriend when I got saved," she explained. "We broke up, but were going back and forth for a while." Olivia had lost her virginity to him and remembers being called a hypocrite for trying to be a Christian and still having sex with her boyfriend. She added, "My boyfriend got a job in another city and asked me to go with him. I asked Jesus what to do. Should I go with him or fully give my life to Christ?"

Olivia didn't go to Chicago with him. She surrendered her life to Jesus. She moved in with a family in the church and joined a full-time discipleship program, where she met her future husband. "I remember he was just stable, kind, and funny. He started asking me for coffee and pursuing a relationship with me."

Dying to Go Forward

To go forward, Olivia felt as though her entire identity had to die. She had to disconnect from the poverty mentality and the fighter persona. "I left my surroundings so radically and went to live with a massively square family who taught me how to live as a Christian," she related. "Even in premarital counseling, they were asking me about my loss of virginity, but I had wholly turned all of that off."

That lifestyle wasn't calling her back, but something else was. "The mentality that kept calling me back was the hustle mentality," she explained. "My mom is a massive, proud hustler who would rather live in her car than get help. I absorbed this mentality and learned how to get what I needed, no matter what. For the longest time, I couldn't see, let alone understand, the Lord as my provider."

Olivia's independence and self-sufficiency negatively affected her marriage. "We've done a lot of therapy, and I've broken through rage, anger, personal instability, and financial instability," Olivia said. "Peace and harmony in the home are vital to me. My husband and I have achieved a sense of safety I never knew growing up."

Olivia is still triggered to go back to a hustling mentality when she feels she's burdening someone. She doesn't want to receive help when she needs it. Or she will only ask for help in a way that doesn't make her seem weak or vulnerable. She struggles with performance and can't stand feeling inferior or not doing a good job.

Olivia's extended family is slowly turning around too. Her mother now believes in Jesus, and her two siblings are coming along. She also led both her father and maternal grandmother to receive Jesus just a few days before they died. Her children, thankfully, do not know violence, poverty, or instability in the home. "They have the stability of a two-parent home, and they know we are committed to serving the Lord," she says.

Olivia hasn't forgotten where she came from. But where she came from was more than just a past; it was a mindset and a spiritual stronghold strategically put in place by demonic forces to keep her bound. To be the first to break free, as Olivia did, takes something extraordinary. It's not simply about working out your salvation; it's about reclaiming a bloodline from years of iniquity and tearing down the familiar spirits that have long believed they have a right to control those who carry that lineage.

The Holy Spirit's Call to "Transitional People"

Whenever I minister in various places, I make it a priority to prepare thoroughly for each venue. I ensure that I am prayed up, ready with a word from the Lord, and covered in prayer by my intercessory teams. On a ministry trip to the Bronx in New York, I was well-prepared with a message for the diverse group of ministers and attendees. Something unexpected happened during the flight, however. I felt a profound sense of the Holy Spirit's presence and clearly heard His voice speaking to my heart. He said just one phrase: *transitional people*. At that moment, I knew exactly what the Lord was prompting me to speak.

When I say *transitional people*, I'm referring to those who are the first in their families to come to Christ. Throughout Scripture, we see examples of such individuals—John the Baptist, the early apostles, and many in the early Church. To be the first means you carry a unique and significant role. You are called to transition your family from the old way of living into a new way in Christ.

As a transitional person, your role is often centered on your family. You're not just walking out your own salvation; you're helping lead your loved ones out of the old and into the new. This means you will reclaim your bloodline and spiritual blessings lost or withheld in previous generations. But because you are the first, you will face unique challenges and spiritual battles. You will experience heightened spiritual warfare as you break generational strongholds and dismantle demonic forces that have held your family captive for years.

If you are such a person, you are called to emerge as the one who ushers in a new season for your family, where Jesus is no longer just a distant figure, but the heavenly Strongman who rules and reigns over your household. You are the vessel God is using to shift the spiritual atmosphere in your family, breaking old patterns and establishing a new legacy rooted in His power and love.

God Gives You Strength for the Turnaround

Here's a verse that captures God's directive to the prophet Ezekiel as He commissioned him to stand firm in the face of a rebellious Israel: "Like adamant stone, harder than flint, I have made your forehead; do not be afraid of them, nor be dismayed at their looks, though they are a rebellious house" (Ezekiel 3:9).

While you may not be a prophet like Ezekiel in the traditional sense, in many ways you are a prophet to your own family. As a transitional person, you are called by God to communicate His Word and principles to your loved ones, guiding them toward a higher way of living. Whether it's your children, grandchildren, or the generations to come, you have the responsibility—and the privilege—to point them to the truth.

I believe that God is imparting to you a holy resilience and a divine stubbornness to stand firm against the pull of old, destructive patterns in your family. As you pave the way for God's transformative work in your household—a task that may span your entire lifetime—understand that this journey will refine you. The weight of this turnaround will feel heavy at times, but in the end, it will turn you into something priceless, like a diamond formed under pressure.

I also prophesy that *you will become the beacon of light in your family, the voice of hope and strength for those who come after you.* The Holy Spirit is speaking this over your life today: *Future generations will look at your life and say, "I want to be just like you."*

Through your faithfulness, you are not just changing your present circumstances; you are setting the course for generations yet to come. Your strength, grounded in God's power, will become the legacy that lights the way for your children and grandchildren—and their children after them.

God Sees Your Family, Past to Future

Have you ever found yourself skimming through those long genealogies in the Bible, like the ones that open up 1 Chronicles? We read, "The descendants of Adam were Seth, Enosh,

Kenan, Mahalalel, Jared, Enoch, Methuselah, Lamech, and Noah" (1 Chronicles 1:1–4 NLT), and the list keeps going. At first glance, these long lists may seem tedious, but they reveal something powerful: God doesn't just see individuals. He sees families—past, present, and future.

These genealogies remind us of something vital: God's vision is generational. He's not just working in your life; He's moving through your entire bloodline. That's why Acts 16:31 (NIV) declares, "Believe in the Lord Jesus, and you will be saved—you and your household." Salvation isn't just personal; it's a promise that extends to your household, your children, your grandchildren, and the generations to come.

Just as God calls individuals, He also calls families. Families are not just random groups of people; they are divine units with specific callings and destinies. Throughout Scripture, we see families anointed for certain assignments. In 1 Chronicles 12:32, we read about the sons of Issachar, "who had understanding of the times, to know what Israel ought to do." This family carried a generational gift of wisdom and discernment, and they led Israel accordingly.

The same is true today. Some families are called to be worshipers and musicians, others to leadership in business or government, and others to ministry or education. When families step into their divine assignment, the anointing flows! And the anointing breaks every yoke, empowering them to fulfill their God-given purpose.

Dr. Michael Maiden once shared an incredible story with our church that still lingers in my mind. When he was eighteen, he was driven by intense zeal for God and spent an entire night in prayer. During that time, he found himself seated at a piano. When his hands touched the keys, he began playing beautifully, without ever being taught. He believed that a dormant bloodline gift had been awakened in him and activated by the unction of the Holy Spirit. That divine anointing didn't stop there, but carried through to some of his children, who also became skilled musicians without training or instruction.[1]

For me, writing has always been a deep calling. I remember finally stepping into book writing with an undeniable pull to write. Then one day, a strange note appeared on my phone—words I hadn't written: "You've received the mantle of the writing sword." With every word I write, I feel that charge surging through me, and it has become my daily rhythm. It wasn't until my third book that I realized this calling was buried deeply in my lineage, dating back to the time of the *Mayflower*. In response to religious persecution and armed with a printing press, members of my family systematically tore apart the Church of England. They have been credited with destroying her religious agenda for America.[2]

Let me prophesy over your family right now: *I believe that God is igniting the anointing and calling on your family. He is reclaiming your family's divine design and putting them into their Kingdom assignment. Many of these blessings and callings were buried under the weight of the curse because those in your family had rebelled and had not yet turned to God. Rebellion against the Lord always carries consequences, impacting the rebellious individual and the generations that follow. Thankfully, God is in the business of restoration. He is restoring your family and bringing them into divine assignment.*

This prophetic encouragement requires a transitional person to stand in the gap and lead the way. It takes perseverance, faith, and a willingness to confront the past in order to restore the future. But God has equipped you for this purpose. He has called you to be the one who turns the tide to break the cycle, and to spark to flame your family's rightful calling.

The Warrior Within: Leaving a Legacy

Transitional people possess a fierce inner strength forged through spiritual warfare. They face life's ordinary challenges, but they also battle generational curses, demonic strongmen and strongholds, familiar demons, and inherited weaknesses that have held their family tree captive for centuries. They are called to fight not just for their own freedom, but for the freedom of future generations.

Scripture shows us that breaking generational bondage requires bold action. Just as the Israelites had to break free from Egypt to ultimately enter their Promised Land, transitional people today must stand against the forces that have kept their families bound to cycles of sin and defeat and out of the blessing. As Paul wrote in 2 Corinthians 10:4 (ESV), "The weapons of our warfare are not of the flesh but have divine power to destroy strongholds."

One woman bravely opened up to me about the painful legacy of incest and abuse within her family for generations. "I experienced profound sexual trauma as a child, resulting in deep rage and bitterness. As an adult, I felt powerless when it came to sexual sin," she reflected. "I couldn't stop a lifestyle of fornication and battled a pornography addiction. It felt like there was no escape."

The Holy Spirit wholly convinced her that her freedom would translate into her children's and grandchildren's freedom, and she began to fight for it. In her intense battle for freedom, she discovered that even the most entrenched challenges could be overcome by the power of the Holy Spirit.

"At a conference during the ministry time, something changed dramatically for me," this woman explained. "It was a very messy scene, but I experienced deliverance from a spirit of perversion."

There was no denying what happened at the conference—that she was delivered from a demon—but she kept cycling into the old mindsets and thought patterns, despite this powerful release. Determined, she fought through it by filling her mind with God's Word and worship. She became accountable for every area of her life and would talk herself through the rough days and moments, using key Scriptures when she felt she was failing. Her hard work has paid off. Today, she is a powerful minister and is actively raising her family in a way that breaks the cycle of pain she once knew. She is truly free from the familiar spirit of perversion and has overcome the mental strongholds too.

Like this woman, transitional warriors are often driven by a deep sense of purpose—fighting not out of bitterness, but out of a calling to redeem their family line. They battle spiritual forces that have plagued their ancestors for generations, and they uproot fear, addiction, and twisted dysfunction. It's not an easy fight, but they know they are not alone. Christ has already won the victory (see 1 John 4:4), and they stand in His authority to break the chains of the past. It's a battle worth fighting because the new legacy they are creating is one grounded in freedom and rooted in God's eternal promises.

People of Repentance—Removing Legal Ground

Transitional people are deeply concerned with repentance for family sins and will intercede to break every curse, in Jesus' name. As Scripture says,

> If My people who are called by My name will humble themselves, and pray and seek My face, and turn from their wicked ways, then I will hear from heaven, and will forgive their sin and heal their land.
>
> 2 Chronicles 7:14

If you haven't done so already, take some quiet time today to meet with your heavenly Father and repent on behalf of your family for every sin you know of that they've committed against Him. While you may not be aware of every transgression, you do know enough to begin the process of repentance. Remember what repentance is. It's a deep, heartfelt turning to God as you acknowledge your sins, your family's sins, and everyone's wrong choices. It's also a war move that removes the legal ground the enemy has been using as a landing strip to attack and oppress you.

You might wonder, *Why do I need to repent for the sins of others? What difference does it make?* Throughout the Bible, we see examples of individuals interceding in this manner for others, repenting on behalf of families, cities, and entire nations. For instance, Ezra's response to the sins of his people is nothing short of profound. When he hears about the sin of the Israelites, even though he hasn't committed this particular sin himself, he doesn't separate himself from it. He spends an entire day in mourning, and then he prays in full identification with his people. He takes their sin upon himself and seeks God's mercy—not just for them, but for *all* of Israel: "O my God, I am too ashamed and humiliated to lift up my face to You, my God; for our iniquities have risen higher than our heads, and our guilt has grown up to the heavens" (Ezra 9:6).

There's incredible power in this kind of repentance—repenting on behalf of others, standing in the gap for the failures of our families and beyond. Ezra's personal act of repentance in Ezra chapter 9 paves the way for the people of Israel to turn their hearts back to God in chapter 10. They mourn their sin, renew their covenant with God, and experience a true spiritual revival.

When you take responsibility for the sins of your family—both past and present—through prayer and the guidance of the Holy Spirit, it creates a powerful spiritual shift. This act of repentance opens the heavens over your unsaved loved ones, making them more receptive to the conviction of the Holy Spirit. It also challenges any legal ground Satan has used to maintain destructive access to your family and loved ones.

Start Breaking Curses

It was podcast day, and if you're a podcaster, you'll totally get this. On podcast day, I step away from the comfort of my home workspace—a space filled with the sounds of my two dogs barking, doorbells ringing with the endless flow of delivery drivers, the hum of neighborhood noises like music, lawnmowers, and even more dogs barking. It's like the whole world is conspiring to interrupt my podcast! So I leave the chaos behind and head to a quieter space. I've found refuge in the back area of our church campus. It's tucked away from the noise, a place where I can record without the world sounding off in the background.

One morning, I pulled into the alley behind the church and parked near the back door. I punched in my code so I could step into the casual meeting space just behind the sanctuary. As I entered, I noticed a man and a woman stretched out on the grass about thirty feet to my left. They looked homeless and worn down, part of a growing number of such people who find themselves in our downtown neighborhoods and business areas. I didn't immediately react because I assumed they'd move on by the afternoon.

But the next week, they were back. And then almost daily. Day after day they camped out, leaving trash, alcohol bottles, and even drug paraphernalia behind. It became clear that they had no intention of moving on, even though nearby agencies could provide help for them. We gently asked them to leave at first, but after days of them staying put, our security team had to take stronger action. Eventually, it was just the man left occupying the space and not the woman, although often others came with him.

We contacted the police repeatedly, but each time, this man found his way back. When he was finally and successfully removed, he settled right across the lot, in a space owned by another building. The owner allowed him to stay, and so the cycle continued. Despite his illegal trespassing, he sat in his lawn chair, mocking us. We kept calling the police, not wanting our families, staff, and children to feel unsafe. This dragged on for over a year, until one day he was just gone. I don't know where he went, but he left.

This experience is a perfect illustration of how curses operate in our lives. Just like that man, curses can linger, refusing to leave—even when they have no right to be there. The curse I'm referring to isn't something mystical or vague; it's a collection of consequences that can result from personal or familial disobedience to God's commands, as outlined in Deuteronomy 28. These curses can grip areas of your life tightly, and no matter how hard you try to break free in your own strength, they will not budge. That's why you need Jesus. What your strength cannot do, He can. Like the woman I told you about who was delivered from the strongman and strongholds of perversion, you can experience freedom when that curse finally leaves. It may feel as if it's stuck, entrenched in your family line, but I want to remind you that in Christ, the curse has no more claim on you.

Don't you agree that it's time to confront those curses? You've been redeemed by Christ, and such curses are not part of your inheritance. Far too often, we mistakenly accept curses as "family traits" or "normal struggles," but through the sacrifice of Jesus, every curse over you has been broken.

Now it's time to take your stand. You are empowered to walk in your victory and challenge anything that does not line up with the truth of your redemption. If something you experience is on the following list, it no longer has authority over you. Jesus paid the price, and it's time to step into freedom.

Look at this list and begin to declare what has already been broken over you. You are not cursed; you are blessed in Christ (see Galatians 3:13, Deuteronomy 28).

- sickness and prolonged illness
- plagues and epidemics

- early death and untimely loss
- helplessness and powerlessness
- destruction and ruin
- mental disorders (like madness or confusion)
- spiritual blindness
- poverty and lack
- being consumed or overwhelmed
- debt and financial bondage
- drought and scarcity
- defeat and failure
- weakness and infirmity
- low status or position
- no sense of safety or security
- unstable relationships
- broken, dysfunctional family
- infertility and barrenness
- homeless and vagabond
- being unloved or unwanted

These curses were broken in Christ. They no longer have the right to hold dominion over your life or your family. As you stand in repentance and intercession, you have the spiritual authority to break these chains, release healing, and see God's restoration flow into your family line. Begin to address these curses like this: *"I break the curse of _____ [destruction, ruin, insanity, poverty, defeat . . . name whatever it is] in my family line. All curses and the demons enforcing them must leave now, in Jesus' name."* And then boldly call forth your generational blessings, which is the topic of my next chapter.

KINGDOM REFLECTIONS

1. When you're the first to break free, you become the *transitional person* in your family. You aren't just working out your salvation; you're walking through a spiritual battlefield to reclaim your bloodline from generational iniquity.

2. When God calls you to be a transitional person, He's not just saving you—He's saving your entire household (see Acts 16:31). This is something you will have to contend for.

3. The path of a transitional person can feel heavy at times, but be encouraged: God gives you supernatural strength for the turnaround.

4. As a transitional person, spiritual warfare will be part of your journey, as will victory. As you stand firm, your faith and perseverance in breaking these cycles will make you a beacon of light for those who come after you.

5. Deliverance isn't just for individuals; it's for families. As the first to break free, you become the deliverer for your family. Stand on the truth that Jesus has already broken every curse. Declare over your life and family, *No more sickness, poverty, destruction, or brokenness, in Jesus' name.*

KINGDOM QUESTIONS

1. Are you the first in your family to come to Christ? If not, do you know someone who fits this role? After reading this chapter, how would you describe the unique purpose and challenges of being this kind of person in a family?

2. Have you ever considered that God sees not only you but your entire lineage—past, present, and future? How does this perspective shift your sense of responsibility toward future generations who may never meet you, but who will inherit the blessings you lay hold of for them?

3. Stubborn, fierce, and relentless—these are traits often found in transitional people. Are you ready to take bold action to reclaim and restore what has been lost in your family?

4. Have you begun the process of repentance on behalf of your family? Why do you think this step is essential for someone stepping into the role of a transitional person?

5. Have you recognized any generational patterns or curses in your family that have been normalized over time? If so, how have you confronted or begun to break free from these patterns?

FIVE

The Power to Restore a Family Bloodline

Growing up, all Mariana knew was chaos. It wasn't just something she lived through; it was woven into the very fabric of her family. The shouting, the fighting, the police raids, and the heartbreak were as constant as the air she breathed. By the time Mariana was old enough to understand the world around her, she had already seen and heard things a child should never have to. She would lie in bed at night, clutching her pillow tightly, tears soaking the material as she prayed for protection, for peace, for silence in a home that knew none of that.

The only reason Mariana knew to pray at all was because of her grandparents. "They were my refuge," she commented. "When my parents couldn't care for me, they did. When life in my parents' house was too much, they welcomed me in."

Her grandfather's home was different. It was filled with the kind of love that didn't hurt. It was quiet enough for her to hear the gentle whispers of the Holy Spirit. Her grandparents took her to church, told her to pray, and reminded her of the promises of God.

But even at her grandparents' house, Mariana couldn't escape the darkness of her family. "My father was a drug dealer, and his life spilled over into ours in devastating ways," she explained. "Weapons were easy access in our home, and I'll never forget the day my little sister accidentally shot herself. She lived, but was horribly injured."

Mariana described how it wasn't unusual to have police storming the house, tearing apart everything they owned, searching for drugs. And yet, her father wasn't someone you could easily hate. He was charismatic, charming, and could make anyone laugh. He had this uncanny ability to make people feel special. To the outside world, they were perfect—beautiful, polished, the picture of a loving family. But behind closed doors, the truth was ugly and violent. Her father's rage often fell on her mother, and the same man who could light up a room would also terrify them all with his threats and fists.

"When I was older, I began to see my father for who he really was, and the admiration I had as a little girl turned into bitterness," Mariana said. "I avoided family trips, stayed with my grandparents whenever I could, and clung to the hope that somehow, God would protect me."

Even amidst the darkness, there were glimmers of something sacred. Mariana's grandfather was in the ministry. "I'll never understand how he could give so much to my dad—enabling him, never holding him accountable—and still have the wisdom to pour into me," she lamented. "But he did. He told me I was special, that God had a plan for me, and that I was not to fear. He didn't know all the ways my father's choices had scarred me, but he saw something in me that even I couldn't see."

Looking back, Mariana realizes how radically God preserved her. He protected her in ways she couldn't comprehend then, setting her apart even when she felt overlooked and forgotten.

Her siblings, however, walked much more complicated paths. Some of them followed in their father's footsteps, protecting his interests and even getting involved in selling drugs for a season. One brother, on the other hand, was churchgoing and was even engaged in ministry for a time—that is, until the day he picked up their father from prison. That moment changed everything for him, and he fell back into the lifestyle they all had fought so hard to escape.

Yet even in their brokenness, God's hand never let go of them. Mariana's brother finally returned to the Lord later in life, a powerful testimony of God's relentless love and faithfulness. Today, Mariana sees the unmistakable hand of God restoring what the enemy tried to steal, rebuilding lives, and reclaiming destinies.

What amazed Mariana the most was how the blessing of ministry, the call to serve God's people, has reappeared in her immediate family. Though her father squandered his gifts, God didn't forget the specific promises made to her grandfather. "Today, all my children walk in that blessing," Mariana said with tears. "God has touched each one in unique ways, and each carries the same love for the church that my grandfather carried, with most being in full-time ministry and all serving in ministry." She added, "It's as if God took the shattered pieces of our family and wove them into a beautiful tapestry of redemption."

Reclaim Your Spiritual Heritage

Generational blessings are real. No matter how far your family seems from God, His promises endure. What was lost in one generation can be reclaimed in the next. Mariana is living proof that God's faithfulness doesn't end with the brokenness of our past. It reaches forward into the future, restoring, healing, and blessing beyond what we could imagine.

Mariana is also a *restorative person*—a lineage reconnector with a divine assignment. Unlike a *transitional person*, who is the first in his or her family to come to Christ, she stepped into the sacred role of reclaiming her family's lost spiritual heritage after a generational gap. *Restorative people* don't just reignite faith in their own generation; they honor the legacy of past believers in their family while boldly rebuilding the spiritual foundation for the future. Mariana carries the mantle of reconnecting her family's faith story, bridging the past with the present, and ensuring that the blessing flows to future generations. This is no small thing—it's a holy mission with eternal impact.

Whether you're a restorative person reigniting your family's spiritual legacy or a transitional person paving a brand-new path of faith, you carry the spiritual authority to usher God's blessings and greatness into your family line. To walk in this authority, you must first grasp the basics of faith and the supernatural power of your words. Once you do, it's time to activate that power through bold declarations and faith-filled decrees. This is how you partner with the Holy Spirit to transform your lineage and secure a legacy of blessing for generations to come.

From the Tongue to Reality

Let me tell you a story about the power of our words and how they can create life or invite chaos. Several years ago, my husband, Ron, decided to test whether our church staff was still engaged with a private Twitter account he had set up for internal communication. It was intended for urgent updates such as medical emergencies or other critical needs within our congregation. Over time, the account had gone quiet, so Ron posted something random to see if anyone was still paying attention: "I won't be at church this Sunday. I was diagnosed with hand, foot and mouth disease."

Of course, this wasn't true! He was trying to see if the team would notice and respond, and thankfully they did. Staff members began calling and checking in. Ron laughed it off, saying, "Oh yeah, I got hand, foot and mouth! Who wants to preach for me on Sunday?" Then he clarified that it was all just a test.

But here's where it gets strange. Within three days, Ron came down with hand, foot and mouth disease—the first adult case his doctor had ever seen! Our three-year-old daughter also caught it, and before long, I ended up with it too. And the impact lingered on my feet for what felt like forever.

What's the lesson here? Words matter. Words create. Proverbs 18:21 couldn't be more precise: "Death and life are in the power of the tongue, and those who love it will eat its fruit." Whether we realize it or not, our words hold power—shaping lives, influencing destinies, and setting things in motion in the unseen realm.

Let's go back to the beginning, Genesis 1. God demonstrated this principle from the start: "And God said, 'Let there be light,' and there was light" (verse 3 NIV). The previous verse tells us that "the Spirit of God was hovering," ready to move, but nothing happened until God spoke. His words carried creative power, and the universe came into being.

Here's a powerful truth: God created us in His image, speaking the world into existence with His words. And we are designed to do the same. Our words carry incredible power, shaping the world around us. That's why we must be intentional about what we speak. Never speak words you don't want to see come to pass. I'm still blown away by how a disease manifested in three days when my husband said he had it.

Think about Jesus. When He cursed the fig tree, it withered from the roots by the next morning (see Mark 11:12–25). When the storm rose up on the sea, He didn't panic or complain; He rebuked it with words: "Peace, be still!" And the storm obeyed (Mark 4:39). Every word Jesus spoke carried heaven's full weight. He healed the sick, raised the dead, rebuked demons, and shifted spiritual atmospheres. And here's the incredible part: We've been given the same authority to speak with heaven's power. In Mark 11:23 (NIV), He says, "Truly I tell you, if anyone says to this mountain, 'Go, throw yourself into the sea,' and does not doubt in their heart but believes that what they say will happen, it will be done for them." God's Word is His will. Speaking in alignment with God's will is not wishful thinking; it's a partnership with the Holy Spirit to bring His will to pass.

Romans 4:17 (NIV) says that Abraham believed in the God "who gives life to the dead and calls into being things that were not." That's what faith does—it speaks unseen realities into existence. When God started speaking to me about ministry in Australia, I remember talking about it, praying about it, and then calling it forth repeatedly. I said it first, again and again, and then I watched it emerge.

So what have you been saying? Are you speaking life or inviting trouble? When we declare God's Word, we're not just talking to the natural world; we're addressing the spiritual realm. Healing, peace, abundance—all of it is activated through faith-filled words. This leads us to discuss declarations and decrees and how to begin making the shift in our families.

Declare and Decree: Do You Know the Difference?

Have you ever heard someone pray and use the phrase, "I declare and decree"? These two words—*declare* and *decree*—hold incredible power in prayer, yet they have distinct meanings. Understanding the significance of each word enables us to unleash their authority more purposefully.

According to *Merriam-Webster*, the word *declare* means "to make known."[1] The Hebrew word *declare* comes from, *achvah*, is further defined as "to set forth an accounting."[2] Consider

The Power to Restore a Family Bloodline

how customs agents ask international travelers, "Do you have anything to declare?" They want to know what you are carrying. Spiritually, declarations are the words we speak into the atmosphere to reveal what we already possess in Christ. When I mention *atmosphere*, I'm referring to the invisible spiritual realm surrounding us, which hosts both demons and angels and is set in motion by our faith-filled words.

Ephesians 3:10 states, "To the intent that now the manifold wisdom of God might be made known by the church to the principalities and powers in the heavenly places." As noted in Ephesians 6:12, these principalities and powers are spiritual beings with whom we wrestle in prayer. Some New Testament examples include Legion, the horde of spirits that possessed the man of the Gadarenes (see Mark 5:1–20), and the slave girl possessed by a "spirit of divination" (see Acts 16:16–18). We know that was a territorial spirit because after Paul cast it out, the entire city came out to fight him (see verses 19–24). When we face spiritual tension and contend in prayer, our words carry the strength necessary for victory over these entities.

Paul outlined our battle this way: "For we do not wrestle against flesh and blood, but against principalities, against powers, against the rulers of the darkness of this age, against spiritual hosts of wickedness in the heavenly places" (Ephesians 6:12).

When the enemy strikes, often through negative thoughts about our identity, we respond with verbal declarations. We declare out loud our righteousness, salvation, eternal victory, and friendship with God. For example,

Enemy: *You're a failure. You're powerless. Success will never happen for you.*

You: "I am victorious in Jesus! I am powerful through the Holy Spirit, and I have what I ask for in

prayer. God's will is my success; it is my prosperity, and I live in the center of His will for my life."

Enemy: *People with a history like yours will never get
better. It's only a matter of time before you go
crazy.*

You: "God has turned it around for my good! I have
the mind of Christ, and I am a new creation.
The old has passed away, and everything is
made new. I am His workmanship and His mas-
terpiece. God has created me for good works in
Christ Jesus."

When we make a declaration, we affirm and reveal what we
already possess in Christ. This is a powerful way to take captive
every thought of defeat, and it puts our spiritual enemies on
notice. Speaking a declaration, however, is different from saying
a decree. When we decree a truth from God's Word, we begin
to establish what has not yet been seen in our lives.

The Supernatural Force of Decrees

We've been born again into God's Kingdom and are fully empowered to be successful in His Kingdom. Everything begins
with prayer, and a power tool for prayer is our ability to "make
a decree." Making a decree causes the blessings of heaven to be
released from heavenly places into our natural realm. We decree
our peace, and we decree our health. We decree salvation to our
families too. We decree favor, wisdom, stability, and success to
our destiny, financial abundance, and more. If God promised
it in His Word, it's ours, and it's "decree-able."

To reiterate, a *decree* is defined as an official order issued
by a legal authority. Naturally speaking, a decision made by

the court's order supersedes the defendant's desire or opinion, whether it's a fine, a denial of driving privileges, or even a jail sentence.

The book of Job declares, "Thou shalt also decree a thing, and it shall be established unto thee: and the light shall shine upon thy ways" (Job 22:28 KJV). The Hebrew word for *decree* in this passage signifies a command that establishes something new and simultaneously cuts down or divides what opposes it.

This is a powerful promise! When you make a decree under the authority of God's Word, it doesn't just bring establishment; it releases divine light that exposes, destroys, and drives out every plan the kingdom of darkness has formed against you. When decrees align with God's will, they unlock breakthroughs, establish His purposes, and illuminate the path ahead with His supernatural favor.

When Decrees Shift Destinies

When Ron and I began pastoring our church, it seemed hopeless and dead. God spoke His plans to our hearts, and we turned them into decrees. We started to say things like these out loud and with authority: "This church is alive! This church is anointed! People are saved, healed, and delivered here! We are reaching cities and influencing nations!"

Keep in mind that this was the exact opposite of what was happening in our church at the time. Either way, these decrees aligned with God's heart and were divinely empowered to bring dead things to life. We remembered that God resurrects the dead and "calls those things which do not exist as though they did" (Romans 4:17). The good news is that in August 1999, the Holy Spirit poured out on a Sunday morning service, a service so powerful that we were never the same again.

When our then-toddler son was diagnosed with a neurological disorder and could barely speak, we did a similar thing. We began to decree the healing promises of God over his life: "By the stripes of Jesus, our son is healed! He is blood-bought, and the curse of sickness is broken, in Jesus' name!"

It didn't happen overnight, but our son's turnaround showed up in second grade, when he began jumping two grade levels at a time. He had been seriously deficient in every testable area up to that point. By the time he was in junior high, however, he was mostly resolved, and by the end of high school, you would never know he had a problem. Today, our son is married and has graduated from college. He shows no signs of speech or comprehension issues. I can't help but reflect on this Scripture: "He sent His word and healed them, and delivered them from their destructions" (Psalm 107:20).

I know a businessman who strongly desired a wife and family. While still single, he purchased a home and felt led to speak into his future with faith and intentionality. Every day, he decreed over his house and thanked God for a loving wife, a thriving family, and a blessed home life. Although none of this was his reality at the time, he saw it clearly in his spirit and decreed it so as to establish it. Not long after, he met the woman who would become his wife. Today, they are happily married, running a successful business together, and raising a beautiful child. Even more remarkable is that their child is the first in many generations on this father's side of the family to be born within the covenant of marriage. This man's faith-filled decrees not only shaped his personal story but also broke a long-standing generational cycle in his family line.

Finally, there was a minister whose husband was diagnosed with cancer—the kind that usually leads to a swift death. Even with treatment, he was given a very short time frame to live. Despite his diagnosis, he continued living, but he wasn't recovering and was in a lot of pain. This couple joined together and began making decrees based on the healing promises in God's Word, and on an unusual prophetic word about his miraculous healing given by a reputable prophet. The minister would decree again and again, "Zachary is cancer-free and will live out the full span of his days! Affliction will not come again!"

A few years later, when this minister's husband returned to the doctor, they could not find any cancer in his body. Praise the Lord.

These testimonies vividly illustrate the power of faith-filled decrees. When we speak into our God-given future, partnering with His promises, we create space for heaven to invade earth. Don't let your circumstances dictate your words. Decree what the Holy Spirit has shown you, and watch as it comes into being.

Decreeing God's Will, Not Personal Agendas

What I write next about decrees is critical and important to pay attention to. Trustworthy decrees will flow from God's written Word and are birthed out of deep communion with Him. Self-serving or manipulative decrees—those rooted in personal agendas rather than God's will—can be spiritually harmful.

We read in Psalm 106:15, "And He gave them their request, but sent leanness into their soul." This verse encompasses the story of the Israelites in the wilderness, who complained and demanded meat despite God providing for them. God granted their request, but also sent a "wasting disease"[3] among them, highlighting the consequence of not being content with God's provision and pursuing personal desires outside His will. This verse is a cautionary tale about the dangers of self-indulgence, selfishness, and entitlement that superimpose God's plans.

Early in our pastoral ministry, for example, an older woman in the church took issue with our shift from hymns to contemporary worship. She was prayerful, but also bitter and controlling. One Sunday, she told my husband she had decreed that our worship pastors "get out of town." He rebuked her on the spot for her sick attitude and blatant disunity. What we didn't realize then was how spiritually dangerous her words were. I talk more about this in *The Intercessors Handbook*, but her bitter decrees opened a door. While people still have choices—and we're not ruled by someone else's words alone—when there's a lack of discernment and a breakdown in holiness, the enemy gains access. That one bitter decree aligned with a dark agenda already at work. The result? The worship pastors' marriage and ministry were destroyed, and their kids were deeply affected.

When we decree, we must ensure that our motives are pure and our words are deeply anchored in Scripture. Decrees are potent tools for partnering with the Holy Spirit, not mechanisms for controlling outcomes to suit our personal preferences.

Understanding the difference between declaring and decreeing is also key. Declarations boldly state God's promises, while decrees carry the authority to establish His will. Together, they help us release God's purposes and establish His Kingdom with precision and spiritual authority in our lives, families, and spheres of influence.

Decrees to Transform Your Family

Do you need help compiling Scripture-based decrees to start the transformation in your family? I've created the following decrees and shared them with many others for their use. When you begin to speak these out loud, you'll feel the power and authority behind them. These aren't just words to say once; you'll want to recite them daily and release your faith as you do, even when opposing circumstances arise. Remember Mark 11:23–24, where Jesus encourages us,

> For assuredly, I say to you, whoever says to this mountain, "Be removed and be cast into the sea," and does not doubt in his heart, but believes that those things he says will be done, he will have whatever he says. Therefore I say to you, whatever things

you ask when you pray, believe that you receive them, and you will have them.

- As for me and my house, we will serve the Lord (Joshua 24:15). We choose His ways, His will, and His Word, and we will walk in His truth.
- I love God and keep His commandments; therefore, the blessings of God rest upon my family for a thousand generations (Deuteronomy 7:9). God's favor and covenant promises are generational, and they are being established in my family line.
- My sons and daughters will prophesy! They will dream dreams and see visions from the Lord (Acts 2:17). The prophetic anointing is upon my household, and the Spirit of God is at work in the lives of my children and grandchildren.
- My family is growing in wisdom, stature, and favor with both God and other people (Luke 2:52). We are walking in the fullness of divine growth and favor, progressing in every area of life.
- Every generational blessing upon my family line will be revealed and stewarded with care. No blessing, talent, gift, or divine ability will be lost, but will be passed down, multiplied, and manifested in this generation and beyond.
- I decree that every family member—now and in the generations to come—will be saved, filled with the Holy Spirit, and serving the Lord. Salvation is their portion, and they will walk in the fullness of God's calling.
- I decree over the men in my family that they will serve the Lord. I decree over the women in my family that they will serve the Lord. I decree over every child, grandchild, great-grandchild, and beyond that they will serve the Lord and be filled with the Holy Spirit.

- I decree that the Holy Spirit is the ruling Spirit of my family, and that Jesus is our heavenly Strongman. I decree that the power of the Holy Spirit will govern every area of our lives, and that the authority of Jesus' name will be a fortress of protection around my family.

KINGDOM REFLECTIONS

1. Generational blessings are real. What was lost in one generation can be reclaimed in the next.

2. A *restorative person* is a lineage reconnector with a divine assignment to reclaim a family's lost spiritual heritage after a generational gap.

3. Whether you're a *restorative person* reigniting your family's spiritual legacy or a *transitional person* paving a brand-new path of faith, you carry the spiritual authority to usher God's blessings and greatness into your family line. To walk in this authority, you must first grasp the basics of faith and the supernatural power of your words.

4. When we make a declaration, we affirm and reveal what we already possess in Christ. This is a powerful way to take captive every thought of defeat, and it puts our spiritual enemies on notice.

5. Speaking a declaration, however, is different from saying a decree. When we decree a truth from God's Word, we begin to establish what has not been seen in our lives yet.

KINGDOM QUESTIONS

1. In establishing or reclaiming a spiritual heritage, what does being a *restorative person* mean versus being a *transitional person*? Which role do you identify with in your family, and why?

2. How did the story of my husband's unintended hand, foot and mouth disease illustrate the principle of Proverbs 18:21 about the power of the tongue? What practical steps can you take to speak life into your circumstances?

3. How do declarations and decrees differ? Why is it important to understand both in prayer?

4. Consider the testimonies shared in this chapter (e.g., the businessman who desired a family, the minister's husband who became well after a cancer diagnosis). How do these examples inspire you to partner with God through decrees in your own life?

5. What warning is presented through the story of the bitter woman's harmful decrees over the worship pastors? How can this example guide your approach to ensuring that your decrees align with God's will?

SIX

Here Comes the New

Aimee Semple McPherson was born on October 9, 1890, in rural Canada, and her life was nothing short of remarkable. She wasn't just an evangelist; she was a trailblazer who embraced the new, pioneering the use of mass media to spread the Gospel of Jesus Christ. Raised by devout Salvation Army parents, Aimee's heart for missions ignited early. At just seventeen years old, she married Pentecostal evangelist Robert Semple, and together they set out for the mission field in China. But tragedy struck and Robert passed away unexpectedly, leaving Aimee widowed and eight months pregnant in a foreign land.

Returning to the United States, she remarried in 1912, this time to Harold Stewart McPherson, who was an accountant. Although they had a child together and settled into domestic life in Pennsylvania, Aimee couldn't ignore her deep and burning call to preach. In 1916, she set out as a traveling missionary, and her bold, Spirit-filled preaching began drawing diverse crowds. People from every background, race, and walk of life were captivated by her anointing.

Aimee's ministry came with many challenges. Her pursuit of God's call cost her another marriage, and then she lost a third to David Hutton for his failure to live a consecrated Christian life. Despite personal setbacks, Aimee pressed on. In Los Angeles, she established her ministry base, Angelus Temple—a massive, concrete-and-steel structure that opened in 1923. It featured the largest dome in North America at the time and became a beacon of Holy Spirit revival. From Angelus Temple, Aimee preached to thousands in person and millions over the airwaves, becoming the first American woman to deliver a sermon on the radio through KFSG, the station she founded.[1]

Aimee's ministry was vibrant, innovative, and compassionate. During the Great Depression, she led charitable outreaches, feeding and clothing those in need and demonstrating the Gospel in action. Aimee wasn't just a preacher; she was a woman of action, a prophetic voice, and a forerunner who embraced new methods to fulfill God's mandate.

It was during one of her early revival tours that Aimee came to Turlock, California, and held at least two powerful meetings.[2] It is believed that those gatherings either sparked a move of the Holy Spirit among a group of believers who had been part of the Turlock Evangelical Free Church, or fanned it into flames. Now filled with the Holy Spirit and speaking in tongues, these believers started meeting regularly for prayer. Their prayer gatherings soon became the Pentecostal Mission and were officially incorporated in September 1917. Over time, this church evolved into Bethel Temple in 1932 and later became Harvest Christian Center in 2001 under my husband's leadership, which was the prophetic name God gave him to signify a future harvest of souls.[3] Today, it's known more simply as Harvest Church, a thriving multicampus ministry that Ron and I have had the privilege of leading for over three decades.

Why am I bringing up Aimee Semple McPherson? Because she was a woman who didn't just embrace the new—she established it. She shattered barriers for women in ministry, pioneered innovative approaches in media, and championed a Spirit-empowered church that transformed both church and Hollywood culture. She wasn't afraid to make a bold statement for the Kingdom, even in the face of controversy. Her legacy paved the way for ministers like me to follow God's call to preach at home and worldwide, using every media platform available.

Aimee's life reminds us that we're not just reclaiming what was lost in our spiritual heritage. We're establishing new blessings, new movements, and new Kingdom realities for generations to come. So as we dive into this chapter, I have to ask: Are you ready to step into the new?

The Breakthrough Principle

As we talk about generational breakthrough, let's look at what I call the *Perez principle*. King David didn't come from just any family line. He came from the house of Perez. That alone should grab your attention. In Ruth 4:8–12, when the elders blessed Ruth and Boaz, they declared, "May your house be like the house of Perez" (verse 12). That wasn't just a poetic blessing. It was a prophetic decree of breakthrough. Then Scripture traces the line of Perez all the way to David: "Now this is the genealogy of Perez: Perez begot Hezron; Hezron begot Ram . . . Obed begot Jesse, and Jesse begot David" (verses 18–22).

Let's unpack this because there's so much more happening here than meets the eye. The name *Perez* literally means "break through,"[4] and his story is rooted in some wild family drama involving Tamar and Judah. Do you know who they are? Tamar wasn't about to sit idly by while her father-in-law, Judah, neglected to fulfill his obligation to her. After the death of her two husbands, both of them the sons of Judah, he was obligated to give her his third son as a husband, but he never did. This left Tamar widowed, childless, and without inheritance or income.[5]

Instead of accepting this injustice, Tamar took bold—and even scandalous—action to secure her place in the lineage of promise. Through an act of deception, she became pregnant by none other than Judah himself. When her pregnancy was revealed, it stirred a holy conviction in Judah. He corrected himself and repented for not fulfilling his obligation. And when she eventually gave birth, it wasn't just one child; it was twins.

Something extraordinary occurred at these twins' birth, which underpins the entire story. While still in the womb, the twins struggled hard against one another. As Zerah began to emerge first, he thrust out his hand, prompting the midwife to tie a scarlet cord around it, saying, "This one came out first" (Genesis 38:28). But then Perez made his surprising move. He pushed past his brother, broke through, and managed to claim the right of the firstborn. Amazed, the midwife exclaimed, "How did you break through? This breach be upon you!" (verse 29). Thus he was named Perez, meaning "break through."

This is what breakthrough in action looked like. Breakthrough isn't tidy, and it often isn't socially acceptable, but it is powerful. And Perez's breakthrough didn't stop with him. His life set a generational trajectory. He became the patriarch of the Perezites—a clan so esteemed that when the Israelites returned from captivity in Babylon, 468 Perezites were chosen to live in Jerusalem. The Bible called all of them "outstanding men" (Nehemiah 11:6 NLT).[6] Can you imagine? A legacy of honor, influence, and leadership—all because one person broke through.

The Prophetic Power of Your Breakthrough

Don't minimize what God is doing in your life right now. That challenge you're navigating? It's not just a trial—it's a divine setup. God is aligning you for a breakthrough that will release freedom, honor, and blessing over your entire family. Your obedience today is the groundwork for your children's inheritance tomorrow.

Catch this in your spirit: When God gives you a breakthrough, He's handing you the authority to rewrite your family's story. Just as the Perezites were honored for generations, your obedience can secure and even establish a new generational blessing.

Step boldly into what God has for you, persist in faith, and allow the Holy Spirit to guide you into your breakthrough moment. Remember, what God does in you isn't just personal—it's prophetic. It will reverberate through your lineage, shaping destinies in ways you can't yet comprehend.

New Wine, New Thinking, New Things

When I stepped into a season of letting go—untangling myself from the familiar and shaking off familiar spirits—things started shifting fast. One of the more significant changes came in my ministry relationships, including some close friendships. Some connections felt as though they naturally faded, while others were painfully torn away. But here's the thing—when *you* change, your relationships will too. When the familiar becomes unfamiliar, not everyone is going to make the transition with you.

Why do we even connect with most people in the first place? It's the familiar. The familiar is a shared mindset, a way of thinking, believing, and speaking. You don't even have to say certain things out loud; you just *know*. But that familiarity also means shared limitations. For example, people operating under a poverty spirit have a specific mindset, even a distinct language. They naturally attract others who think and speak the same way. And yes, familiar spirits are behind a lot of it, keeping the cycle going. On the flip side, those who walk in biblical prosperity—both spiritually and materially—carry a completely different mindset and language, drawing like-minded people into their world.

What happens when you start breaking free from those limiting mindsets? Changes in your relationships are inevitable. Breaking free isn't just about leaving a group or a place; it's about leaving a mentality. Look at Abraham. God told him, "Get out of your country, from your family and from your father's house, to a land that I will show you" (Genesis 12:1). Why? Because if Abraham had stayed in the familiar, it would have sabotaged his destiny. The same goes for us. Familiar might *feel* safe, but it can strangle what God is trying to do in your life.

I'll never forget how God used Isaiah 43:19 to navigate me through my own transition: "Behold, I will do a new thing, now it shall spring forth; shall you not know it? I will even make a road in the wilderness and rivers in the desert." God is always doing something new, but stepping into it requires a mindset shift. Jesus put it this way: "And no one puts new wine into old wineskins; or else the new wine bursts the wineskins, the wine is spilled, and the wineskins are ruined. But new wine must be put into new wineskins" (Mark 2:22).

Here's how I see it: Wine represents something that impacts your thinking. The old wine in this passage? Old mindsets. The new wine? A fresh way of thinking. And let me tell you, you cannot take a new way of thinking and force it into an old framework. It just won't work.

When my husband and I first started pastoring, there was this massive pipe organ in the sanctuary. We were very young pastors and were ready to see worship come alive. Our first priority was shifting the music from traditional to something that carried the sound of revival. People were fixated on holding their hymn books and singing straight from the pages, with no real desire to connect with the Holy Spirit. We wanted guitars, drums, and an atmosphere that invited His presence. Leading contemporary worship with a pipe organ in the background sent the wrong message. It had to go.

And that wasn't the only shift we had to make. We've *constantly* had to challenge old paradigms to make room for the new. Even now, as technology and ministry methods evolve through broadcasts, simulcasts, and online platforms, we're always rethinking the wineskin to steward growth, while staying anchored in the Word and the move of the Spirit. It's a tension point, but it's necessary.

In life and in ministry, it's way too easy to get comfortable with the familiar. And if we're not careful, that comfort turns into a monument to the past. We have to stay open and highly flexible, and keep making room for the *new thing* God is doing, because what worked yesterday will not work today.

Discerning an Opportunity in the New

When Facebook first emerged, I jumped right in without hesitation. I immediately sensed its potential and couldn't stop exploring everything about it. Of course, not everyone around me shared my enthusiasm. Some gave me *that look*—you know, the one that says, *Are you sure you're not stepping onto the devil's turf?* I could only shake my head and wonder why they didn't see what I saw.

Back then, Facebook was just a social network for college students that Mark Zuckerberg started while attending Harvard. It followed other platforms like Friendster, AOL, and Prodigy. I had a brief run with Prodigy back in my journalism days at Oral Roberts University, but let's just say the department didn't love the unexpected expenses that came with my creative networking attempts. Myspace? I tried it but didn't really connect with it. Then Facebook opened to the public, and something about its ease of connection felt significant. I knew it was different.

Now, I'll admit that Zuckerberg didn't have the most glowing reputation. He was known as a tech genius who bent the rules, bucked ethics, and hacked his way to success. Despite the controversy, I wasn't about to let that stop me. I could feel in my spirit that this platform had incredible potential, and I didn't want to miss it.

Looking back, I've noticed something about God's people and new technology. Every generation seems to greet innovation with suspicion. The religious mindset often gives anything new the side-eye, but if you're paying attention to the Holy Spirit, you'll recognize that God can use these tools for His glory. That's exactly what happened with Facebook for me. I was still finding my way in ministry, but I refused to let fear or criticism hold me back. I knew God could use this.

Fast-forward to now, and we've seen Facebook evolve in ways both good and bad. But in its earlier days, it became a game changer for me and my ministry. Facebook allowed me to connect with people far beyond my local church. It gave me a platform to test and refine the message God was building in me.

For example, much of my book *Seeing the Supernatural* was birthed through Facebook. I posted short statements about the gift of discerning of spirits and gauged how people responded. One of those posts became the phrase that resonated with so many: *"You're not crazy. You have a gift!"* That single statement gave countless sensitive discerners a sense of identity and purpose around a challenging spiritual gift. Those posts eventually became the book's foundation, impacting tens of thousands worldwide. It's amazing how God can use something simple to transform many lives.

This is what it means to embrace the new: Recognize where God is moving and step into it without fear or hesitation. Don't let skepticism or criticism hold you back. Be bold, and stay Spirit-led.

Stepping into Greater Works

Newness isn't just about technology; it's about how God is moving in fresh and miraculous ways. I think I understand a little more why Jesus told us, "You will do greater works than Me" (see John 14:12). He wasn't just talking about quantity; He was pointing to the new and greater ways His power would manifest in each generation. Take Acts 19:11–12 as an example: "Now God worked unusual miracles by the hands of Paul, so that even handkerchiefs or aprons were brought from his body to the sick, and the diseases left them and the evil spirits went out of them." Imagine how unconventional and new that was for their time! And yet, it worked because God was moving in a way they hadn't seen before.

Now, fast-forward to our time. Who could have imagined the kinds of miracles we're seeing today? Miracles flowing through the intersection of faith, science, and technology. For instance, I know of healing ministers God is using to supernaturally turn metal implants in people's bodies back into bone during healing meetings. Think about it—there weren't even metal implants in Paul's day. This is a miracle uniquely designed for our time.

I've also witnessed supernatural financial deposits showing up in people's bank accounts during meetings, and individuals receiving miracle gold fillings, but always on their back wisdom teeth. (By the way, I'm unsure why gold fillings only appeared on back teeth, but I'm thankful they never show up in the front.) I've seen supernatural hair restoration on women, as well as supernatural weight loss. One woman instantly lost so much weight in a meeting that she had to leave and get a change of clothes. At our church, we see healing miracles every week, many of which occur during our corporate worship times, without anyone laying hands on the person. We often see healing miracles in our online formats too.

These are the miracles of our time, reflecting the unique ways God is moving right now. They challenge us to expand our faith and embrace the new expressions of His power. He's still doing the impossible, but doing it in ways that align with what this generation needs.

Stepping into Global Ministry Now

The same applies to ministry. Today, global ministry can happen almost instantly. We no longer need to wait for an invitation to preach the Gospel; we can engage on any number of social media platforms and share our personal testimony of salvation, and we can do it instantly. The result? The globe shows up.

This kind of instant engagement is a sign of the times. Jesus said, "This gospel of the kingdom will be preached in the whole world as a testimony to all nations, and then the end will come" (Matthew 24:14 NIV).

I also believe the speed at which we can now share the Gospel reflects the urgency of Christ's return—even the need for discipleship on a global level. For example, I've been mentoring thousands of individuals for almost a decade online and engaging in online healing, prophetic ministry, and even deliverance ministry.

The Perez Principle in Families

The new that God is doing isn't just about technology, miracles, or ministry; it's also showing up in our families. The reality is that family change doesn't happen at the speed of technology. It's slow, messy, and downright uncomfortable at times. This is where the wineskin change gets personal. It demands transformation—not just surface-level adjustments, but deep heart work, a shift in thinking, and the breaking of ingrained beliefs.

Restoring generational blessings and reclaiming a lost spiritual heritage is no small feat. Let's call it what it is: a monumental task. This kind of restoration doesn't happen overnight. It takes years, sometimes lifetimes, to undo the damage and rebuild. But there's good news—Isaiah 43:19 gives us a vision of hope: "Behold, I will do a new thing, now it shall spring forth; shall you not know it? I will even make a road in the wilderness and rivers in the desert." This verse reminds us that God's new thing doesn't look like what we're used to. It's not going to fit neatly into our old boxes. It's the kind of new that shocks the system—a river where there's been nothing but dry land, a road carved out of the wilderness. It's unexpected, disruptive, and undeniably God.

Take, for example, the rise of apostolic and prophetic partnerships in marriages. Let's just say this isn't your typical "two shall become one" scenario. These couples are waking up to the reality that their union was crafted in heaven, with a Kingdom mandate in mind. Now, enter the Perez principle—a concept of sudden breakthrough, a divine breaking forth that establishes a new familial blessing. God is using these marriages to bulldoze through generational patterns and release a fresh expression of His design for family and ministry. Every step such couples take together brings forth something new because their union carries a unique blueprint for this generation.

When my husband and I got married, we had no idea of the depth of what God was up to. Like everyone else, we were just two people trying to figure it out. But over time, we've come to see that our union wasn't just about us; it was about a divine purpose. And we're not alone. God is raising up apostle and prophet couples who are reshaping family legacies and releasing a Kingdom movement in and through His Church.

But here's the thing: Stepping into the new means you've got to let go of the old. Let's be honest, the old feels cozy, doesn't it? It's predictable and manageable. But Jesus was crystal clear—new wine needs new wineskins. If you cling to what's familiar, you'll miss what God is trying to do. It's like the Israelites whining about Egypt. Really? They were begging to go back to slavery because they couldn't handle the discomfort of the wilderness. They wanted the easy road, but God was offering them the Promised Land.

Let's not make the same mistake. If we resist the new, we'll end up wandering, stuck in yesterday's season while God is trying to move us forward. Embracing the new takes guts. It takes faith. And it takes the willingness to trust that the God who makes rivers in deserts and roads in wildernesses knows exactly where He's leading us.

Shattering Ceilings Is Your Assignment

At times, I drive past a church that outright forbids women from doing anything close to the kind of ministry that I do. And every time, I can't help but think, *If the women in that church had even a spark of calling burning inside them, they'd hop a few blocks over and let God sort things out.*

It's true that I've taken plenty of cues from one of our church's founding catalysts, Aimee Semple McPherson. As a woman in ministry, I've had my fair share of ceilings to shatter. I was probably the first female itinerant preacher in my city, not to mention an ordained minister, and I authored several books in multiple languages. We're a smaller city and a bit slow to change the wineskin when it comes to church traditions. And while there might be a handful of women pastors here now, I'm one of the few—and maybe the only one—preaching globally at this level. I say none of this out of comparison or pride. I can't even say I have the ability on my own to do this, because I know that I don't. Every day, I commit myself to God and do His work, and this is how my life has spilled out.

Let me tell you something if you are a woman: Breaking barriers is part of your God-given assignment. Remember the daughters of Zelophehad? These five sisters didn't settle for the hand they were dealt (see Numbers 27:1–11). Their father had died in the wilderness, with no sons to inherit his land. At that time, only men could inherit property, and these women faced a major problem: no father, no brothers, no inheritance, no future.

But did these ladies sit around sulking? Absolutely not. They marched right up to Moses, Eleazar the priest, the leaders, and the congregation at the tent of meeting—a bold move for women back then. They said, "Why should our father's name disappear from his clan because he had no son? Give us property among our father's relatives" (Numbers 27:4 NIV).

This had never been done before, so Moses brought their case before the Lord. And guess what? God ruled in their favor: "What Zelophehad's daughters are saying is right. You must certainly give them property as an inheritance among their father's relatives" (verse 7 NIV). These women not only changed the rules but also paved the way for others.

Here's the lesson: Ceilings are often just in your mind. Some barriers are generational, some cultural, but if God's hand is on it, *they will break*. The same spirit of faith that fueled those bold sisters is alive in you. So stop letting *No* be the final word. If you're called, step up, speak out, and watch God make a way.

I think of a woman I met at a small conference in the Midwest. She came from a strict religious background and knew I'd been born again in a similar denomination. She admitted that she struggled with their rules. Hearing my story is what gave her the courage to step into freedom. She began to see herself as God intended, outside all those man-made regulations. And while I'm no feminist (let's be real, I'm all about Kingdom alignment), I do love this quote from well-known historian Laurel Thatcher Ulrich, who has written some amazing books about women of the past: "Well-behaved women seldom make history."

As for me, I've taken the Lord's instruction to *call in the new*. I even made a decree list about new things that I declare almost daily. (It's in appendix B, if you want to peek.)

So what's ahead for you? What generational blessings need to be reclaimed, and what new ones need to be established? In this fast-paced, tech-driven world, let's not forget that God's Word is timeless. If you want to stake your claim in your family and future, start by understanding His principles. And here's a word of wisdom to prep you for the next chapter: Don't be quick to walk away from your marriage. Build it strong; it's part of your inheritance. If you are married, it's the catalyst that releases everything we are talking about in this book.

KINGDOM REFLECTIONS

1. Your breakthrough today has prophetic power—not just for you, but to establish generational blessings for your descendants.

2. God uses challenges as divine setups, aligning you for breakthroughs that will impact your family's future and rewrite your legacy.

3. Obedience in the present prepares the groundwork for your children's inheritance. It establishes a new generational trajectory.

4. Breaking free from familiar spirits and the old mindsets that fueled them is essential for stepping into new blessings and moving forward in God's plan.

5. Shattering ceilings is your assignment. Some barriers are generational and some are cultural, but they will break because God's hand is on you for this.

KINGDOM QUESTIONS

1. What pioneers in history have inspired you, and why?
2. The history of Perez is both messy and scandalous. Does this give you hope that God can turn any situation around for good?
3. What are your thoughts in the light of this statement? "It's not just a trial—it's a divine setup. . . . When God gives you a breakthrough, He's handing you the authority to rewrite your family's story."
4. Are your relationships based in the familiar? As you embrace God's future for you, is it possible that your relationships will change?
5. What ceilings has God assigned you to break?

SEVEN

Fight for Your Marriage

Shara was preparing for an international ministry trip when something unsettling caught her attention. Her husband had been texting with a woman—someone loosely connected to his extended family—about business dealings in an East African country she was about to visit. "I didn't like the tone of their exchanges and brought it up, but instead of clarity, I got a defensive reaction," she explained. His anger at her questions left her feeling even more unsettled.

On her flight, Shara had a vivid, prophetic dream that clarified everything. In the dream, God revealed a woman who seemed to have an inappropriate interest in her husband. She saw herself confronting the woman boldly, engaged in a fierce spiritual battle. "I took charge in the dream, fighting her off with authority," Shara explained. "Then God began revealing more people tied to this situation, exposing what I was really up against."

But as the dream unfolded, something shifted. The woman in the dream began to gain strength and came after her instead. Startled awake, Shara immediately heard the voice of God: *You have to fight.*

She resisted. *I just want to be free, Lord*, she remembers saying. *Why do I have to fight again?*

This wasn't the first time she had dealt with women crossing boundaries with her husband, and every instance traced back to their connections in foreign countries. Though she had no concrete evidence of infidelity, these repeated situations had eroded her trust.

Through prayer and discernment, Shara began to perceive the deeper spiritual dynamics at work. Like several foreign nations, the one she was visiting also contends with strongholds tied to ancestral and family idols. These include *spirit spouses*—demonic entities that claim ownership of a person, behaving like a jealous spouse and operating sexually in dreams. Shara recognized these patterns from her own upbringing. Her mother's family had been spiritually "married" to a demonic entity—a marine spirit, as it was often called in their country. These spirits would manifest through disturbing sexual dreams, leaving spiritual destruction in their wake.

Shara had been delivered from these highly possessive spirits years ago, but she knew they always waited for an opportunity to reenter. "I've seen their influence firsthand," she said. "Some of my extended family members are visibly possessed and actively communicate with these spirits. This isn't a metaphor. It's a real spiritual battle deeply entrenched in the culture."

During her short missionary trip, Shara tried to focus on the work at hand. But God had other plans. An evangelist shared a testimony about how God had healed his marriage, and his words pierced her heart. That night in her hotel room, Shara had a powerful encounter with the Holy Spirit. "God gave me the strength to face my pain and stop pushing my marital problems aside," she said.

Just prior to returning home, things escalated. Her children called to tell her that her husband was planning to take an international trip, even transferring money and preparing to take over his family's affairs. Within days, Shara was in court seeking a legal separation—not to end her marriage, but to protect her home and children.

"I felt God's presence in the courtroom," she said. And then something unexpected happened. Her husband had a sudden change of heart and canceled his trip. In the midst of this turmoil, God gave Shara another dream. She saw her husband reading his Bible and fully surrendering to Christ. "That dream gave me hope to endure the process," she said.

As Shara pressed into the Holy Spirit, she realized this battle wasn't just about her marriage; it was about the call of God on her life and the spiritual legacy in their children. Her husband's family had deep ties to ancestral idols and witchcraft, and as the eldest son, he was being drawn back by the familiar spirits into these traditions. If these spirits succeeded, they would come looking for this couple's children too. But God was saying, *Not on your watch, Shara!*

"I began to understand that my assignment on my ministry trip wasn't just about ministry; it was about breaking generational strongholds in my husband's family. This battle wasn't just personal; it was spiritual and had eternal significance."

Shara recalled a dream from the night of their wedding. A demon idol had appeared, staring at her as if sizing her up. She didn't fully understand it then, but now she does. The enemy had recognized her calling before she even realized it. God had positioned her in this family not only to bring them back to Him but to shift the spiritual atmosphere over an entire territory.

"This journey has been anything but easy," Shara said, "but I see now that God is using it to refine me. He's teaching me to be a better wife, a more attentive intercessor, and a bold cursebreaker." And as for the legal separation case? The court disqualified it. "God isn't done with my marriage. He's using it for His glory."

Marriage: God's Original Blueprint

From the very start, marriage was God's idea. Adam and Eve weren't just the first humans. They were the blueprint for every marriage that followed. Genesis 2:24 is crystal clear: "A man shall leave his father and mother and be joined to his wife, and they shall become one flesh." Don't miss this—God Himself officiated the very first wedding in the Garden of Eden. He didn't just bring the first couple together on a whim; He designed them to be united in spirit, soul, and body. That's a covenant, my friend.

And make no mistake—*a covenant is no casual contract.* It's a sacred, unbreakable bond anchored in God's unchanging nature and His unwavering faithfulness. When God makes a covenant, He means business. It's lasting, it's holy, and it reflects His commitment in the strongest possible way. That's the foundation He laid for marriage—one that's about *holiness ever after*, not just *happily ever after*.

As author and scholar Dr. Dennis Kinlaw put it, "Human sexuality is a far more sacred thing for God's followers and a far more significant thing in God's eyes than most of us have dreamed. Perhaps this is why God takes our sexual conduct so seriously."[1]

Now, here's where it gets real. Sexuality, believe it or not, becomes *Paul's prophetic lens* for understanding the Church as the Body of Christ. Christ is the Groom, and His Church is the Bride. This is the divine romance, the heavenly union that shakes the very foundations of what it means to love. In

Ephesians 5:22–33, Paul drops truth bombs about how husbands should love their wives—and trust me, he's not playing around. He points directly to the cross, the ultimate symbol of sacrificial love, where Christ laid it all down for His Bride. That's the gold standard. Christ's love for His Church isn't just a feeling. It's a covenant, a promise sealed in blood.

Paul doesn't stop there. He layers in another metaphor: *the body*. The Church as the Body of Christ (see Ephesians 5:28–33). This isn't just poetic language; it's prophetic revelation. When Paul pulls in Genesis 2:24, he's not just quoting an old Scripture; he's unveiling a deep mystery. He's showing us that the marital union reflects the essence of the Church. It's radical. It's sacred. And it's the love story that defines all others.

Allow this truth to sink in, because it has the power to shatter your understanding of the Church and elevate your view of Christ's love to a whole new level.

I remember an unmarried couple who had been living together for decades. They also had children together. One day, the woman asked me, "Why get married now? What's the point after all this time?"

I told her, "By getting married, you're making a powerful statement to God, and to the spiritual realm, your kids, and even your grandkids. You're telling them you're in a godly covenant. You're saying you're not fornicating anymore."

They got legally married within a month—and I believe curses were broken right there.

Marriage as Covenant: The Sacred Union

Marriage isn't just a concept tucked into the pages of the Bible. It's a divine cornerstone, a sacred covenant so deeply embedded in the Hebrew mindset that by the time we hit the New Testament, no one even needed to explain it. They just *got it*. But when we grasp how sacred marriage is to God, something shifts inside us. It moves our perspective from casual to consecrated, from ordinary to extraordinary.

Let this sink in: History began with a wedding in Eden. Jesus kicked off His miracle-working ministry at a wedding in Cana. And the ultimate crescendo? The Marriage Supper of the Lamb in the New Jerusalem. Are you seeing the pattern? Marriage is the thread God has woven through His eternal story line, from beginning to end.

For that reason, God doesn't take covenant faithfulness lightly. And when it came to the prophet Hosea and the Israelites, He enforced this point well. Imagine God telling you to marry someone you *know* will break your heart. That's precisely what happened when God told Hosea to marry a promiscuous woman: "Go, marry a promiscuous woman and have children with her, for like an adulterous wife this land is guilty of unfaithfulness to the LORD" (Hosea 1:2 NIV). Can you imagine the emotional toll? But God had a point. He wanted Hosea to live out the heartbreak God Himself felt over Israel's unfaithfulness. This wasn't just obedience; it was painful obedience.

Ezekiel takes the marriage metaphor up a notch with a raw, unfiltered narrative (see Ezekiel 16). He describes Israel as an abandoned infant—unloved, unwanted, and left to die. But God saw her, nurtured her, and cherished her. When she grew up, He declared, "You became Mine" (Ezekiel 16:8). It's the ultimate love story. But instead of faithfulness, Israel chose infidelity and began chasing after other gods. It wasn't just disobedience; it was covenant betrayal. And when Israel turned to idols, God didn't mince words. He called it what it was: prostitution and harlotry. Those words aren't just dramatic. They carry a spiritual weight. Israel wasn't just breaking a rule; she was shattering a sacred bond.

Jeremiah adds his voice, recalling Israel's honeymoon phase with God: "I remember the devotion of your youth, how as a bride you loved me" (Jeremiah 2:2 NIV). Then Isaiah wraps it up with a breathtaking promise of restoration: "No longer will they call you Deserted . . . but you will be called Hephzibah, and your land Beulah; for the LORD will take delight in you, and your land will be married" (Isaiah 62:4 NIV). Did you catch that? *Hephzibah* means "My delight is in her," and *Beulah* means "married." God's love for His people is so extravagant that He uses wedding language to describe their redemption.

Here's the kicker: This metaphor wasn't a prophetic innovation. It goes all the way back to Sinai. When God made a covenant with Israel, it wasn't just legal or political; it was personal. It was a marriage. God wasn't drafting a contract; He was taking a Bride. That's why in Deuteronomy 31:16 (NIV), God warned Moses, "These people will soon prostitute themselves to the foreign gods of the land they are entering. They will forsake me and break the covenant I made with them." Israel's idolatry wasn't just rebellion; it was spiritual adultery.

So when you look at the Sinai covenant (see Exodus 19–20), don't just see it as a legal agreement. See it for what it really is: God's wedding day with His chosen people.

Faithfulness Is More Than Not Cheating

I'll never forget one Sunday morning when I walked into the sanctuary before service. There she was—well-dressed, sitting near the front, holding court with a little group of women. But instead of preparing her heart for worship, she was quietly tearing her husband apart. She wasn't loud, but she might as well have been, the way her words cut like daggers. As I listened, I thought, *Lady, a lot of women would love to be married to your husband. You're the problem here, not him.*

Sure enough, this couple divorced soon after, and both of them remarried. What a tragedy, and not just for them, but for their kids. That's the kind of legacy no one wants to leave behind.

Let me say this loud and clear: *Faithfulness in marriage is much more than not cheating!* It's about guarding your words, your attitudes, and your actions. When God says in Malachi 2:14–16, "I was there when you made your vows" (my paraphrase), He isn't just making a casual observation. He's issuing a serious reminder. He's saying, *I heard every promise you made, and I'm holding you to it.* Faithfulness is about honoring the covenant, not just with your body, but with your whole being—your heart, your mind, your words, and your behaviors.

And here's the thing: Unfaithfulness isn't just about infidelity. It's also strife. It's pride. It's verbal abuse, emotional neglect, hatefulness, and irresponsibility. It's walking into the house, seeing your spouse, and acting as if he or she is invisible. It's saying, "*I love you*," but living as if you don't. Faithfulness isn't just what you do; it's the *how* behind it. It's showing up for your marriage every day, fully present, fully invested, and fully committed to being the best version of yourself in that covenant.

When Pride Takes Root, Love Fails

God gets fiery about the marriage covenant in Malachi 2:14–16 because it matters to Him and it should matter to us. Why? Because marriage is a reflection of God's covenant love, and the enemy hates anything that mirrors God's glory. Satan is always on the prowl, looking for ways to corrupt or divide what God has joined together. And let's not kid ourselves, the enemy is crafty. He doesn't just come in through the big stuff like adultery; he slips in through the small cracks—the unresolved argument, the harsh word, the cold shoulder, the *I'll get back at you* attitude.

When we allow bitterness, pride, or neglect to take root, we're not just making a relational mistake; we're opening spiritual doors. And let me tell you, those doors don't stay empty for long. The enemy thrives in environments of dishonor and division. When you leave those cracks open, you're inviting curses and spiritual strongholds into your marriage and family.

I've seen it happen, even to those who should've known better. There was this power couple in ministry who had it all: a multisite church, a healing and counseling center, books, media resources, international projects, and conferences with top-tier speakers. On the surface, they were the picture of success. But behind the scenes? A hot mess. They owned multiple homes but could barely stay in one house together. Their fights were legendary.

It all came crashing down when she refused to fix publicly what he thought she had mishandled. That's what I heard anyway, although I never confirmed it. But even if it's true, was that really the thing that broke them? Probably not. As my husband always says, "It's never the worst thing you did. It's the last thing you did."

The real issue? Pride. As the saying goes, they were both as proud as hell itself, and Scripture is clear: Destruction always follows pride (see Proverbs 16:18).

Their divorce wasn't just painful for them. It was catastrophic for everyone connected to them. Their kids, grandkids, church members, ministry partners, ministry school students—so many lives were impacted by their broken covenant. And here's the thing: What God intended to be a generational blessing turned into a generational curse. Instead of a legacy of faith, they left behind a trail of heartbreak and confusion.

Theirs is an extreme example, but it's a sobering one. Marriage is sacred, and it's worth fighting for—not just for your sake, but for the generations to come. So shut those cracks, deal with the small stuff before it becomes big stuff, and guard your covenant as if your life depends on it. Because spiritually speaking, it does.

Faithfulness in marriage is about more than avoiding the obvious pitfalls; it's about being vigilant to guard the covenant. It's about recognizing that the enemy isn't just after your happiness; he's after your legacy. He knows that if he can destroy your marriage, he can wound your children and sow seeds of dysfunction for generations to come. Legacy and generational blessings are so important to God that He assigned an ancient prophet to facilitate them on earth.

The Spirit of Elijah Prevents a Curse

Every Jewish Seder meal has a cup of wine and a chair set aside for Elijah the prophet. It's a beautiful tradition, but let's be honest, Elijah isn't showing up just for a drink or to admire the table setting. He's on a mission from God to restore what's broken, turn hearts, and release blessings. That chair isn't just a symbol of hope; it's a prophetic reminder that Elijah's ministry is alive and active today, and it's time we lean into it.[2]

Elijah wasn't a passive prophet. He didn't slide into Mount Carmel with a polite sermon and a prayer. No, he called fire down from heaven, tore down the idols, and rebuilt the altar of the Lord with his own hands. He called the people of Israel out of their spiritual double-mindedness and brought them back into covenant with God. But the prophet Malachi highlights an even deeper, weightier aspect of Elijah's ministry, one that strikes at the very heart of generational restoration:

> Behold, I will send you Elijah the prophet before the coming of the great and dreadful day of the LORD. And he will turn the hearts of the fathers to the children, and the hearts of the children to their fathers, lest I come and strike the earth with a curse.
>
> Malachi 4:5–6

Did you catch that? If this restoration doesn't happen, God says He will strike the earth with a curse. That's not just a warning; it's a wake-up call. The connection between fathers and children—parents and the next generation—is critical. When these hearts are turned away from one another, curses take root. But when restoration comes, those curses are shattered, and generational blessings are released like a flood.

Some of us are standing in the middle of a spiritual battlefield in our families and wondering why things feel so chaotic. The enemy's strategy has always been to divide generations because he knows that when families are fractured, curses flourish. But God's plan is bigger, stronger, and more glorious. He's turning hearts right now—between fathers and sons, mothers and daughters, spiritual parents and their spiritual children—because heaven's blessings are waiting to be poured out.

And let's not pretend that honor isn't part of this equation. God made it clear in the Ten Commandments: "Honor your father and your mother, that your days may be long upon the land which the LORD your God is giving you" (Exodus 20:12). Honor isn't just about being polite at Thanksgiving dinner; it's a spiritual principle that activates blessings and shuts the door on curses.

This goes beyond biological families too. It's about the Church and the spiritual generations coming together. The older generation has a vital role: to make room for the new, even when the new's methods seem messy or unconventional. And younger leaders? Don't dismiss those who've fought hard to get us here. Instead, honor them! There's a double portion of blessing waiting for you when you value and respect the ones who paved the way. That's where breakthrough happens—curses are broken, and blessings flow like never before.

Now, let's talk about *your* marriage, because honestly, that's where this all starts. If you're not fighting for your marriage, the enemy is already winning. Your marriage is the foundation for generational blessings. It's where legacy is built or broken. So stop tolerating dysfunction, stop letting bitterness fester, and stop letting the enemy write your family's story. When you fight for your marriage, you're fighting for your children, your grandchildren, and every generation that comes after you. You're decreeing, "This is where the curse ends and the blessing begins!"

Elijah Versus the Spirit of Jezebel

This battle for marriage? It's more than just personalities clashing, or unmet expectations between two people. It's spiritual warfare, plain and simple. Just as the spirit of Elijah is sweeping across the earth, restoring families and reconciling hearts, there's a demonic counterpart bent on destruction—the spirit of Jezebel.

Let's talk about Queen Jezebel. Her story is found in 1 and 2 Kings, and trust me, it's not pretty. Jezebel wasn't just a spoiled princess; she was the daughter of Ethbaal, a king and priest of Baal—a god whose worship practices were as twisted as they come. Think grotesque, lewd, and utterly vile. When she married King Ahab of Israel, she didn't just come with her luggage; she brought her Baal-worshiping agenda. And let me tell you, Ahab rolled out the red carpet for it, leading all Israel into spiritual chaos.

But then there was Elijah. This fiery prophet didn't back down. He challenged Jezebel and her Baal-worshiping posse to a showdown on Mount Carmel. Yahweh showed up, fire fell from heaven, and God's power made it crystal clear who the real King of kings is. Yet despite the dramatic display, Jezebel dug her heels in. Instead of repenting, she doubled down, vowing to kill Elijah.

Here's the kicker: Jezebel's refusal to submit to God's power and authority led to her violent demise. Elijah prophesied it: "The dogs shall eat Jezebel by the wall of Jezreel" (1 Kings 21:23). And guess what? That's exactly what happened. Her end wasn't just tragic; it was a prophetic exclamation point!

Just to reiterate, the spirit of Elijah isn't just a story from the past. It's a mantle of restoration and reconciliation that is active in the earth today. Malachi 4:5–6 reveals Elijah's on-going assignment: to turn the hearts of fathers to their children and the hearts of children to their fathers. It's a spiritual force aimed squarely at healing families and restoring covenant relationships.

But Jezebel? Oh, she's about the exact opposite. The Jezebel spirit's agenda is to sever covenants, pervert worship, and dismantle families. This spirit hates godly authority, despises covenant love, and thrives on manipulation and domination. This spirit is anti-family, anti-covenant, and anti-God. And don't miss this: While the spirit of Elijah moves to restore, the spirit of Jezebel moves to destroy, seduce, and enslave.

Fast-forward to the book of Revelation, where Jezebel's influence takes on an even larger, more sinister role. John describes a spirit principality he calls the "great harlot," one that corrupts kings and nations alike: "Come, I will show you the judgment of the great harlot who sits on many waters, with whom the kings of the earth committed fornication, and the inhabitants of the earth were made drunk with the wine of her fornication" (Revelation 17:1–2).

Sound familiar? This is Jezebel on a global scale. She's not just after individuals or families; she's gunning for entire nations, luring them into spiritual adultery and rebellion against God. But here's the good news: *Greater is He who is in us than he who is in the world* (see 1 John 4:4).

The spirit of Elijah is alive and active, breaking curses and releasing blessings over families, marriages, and generations. The battle is fierce, but the victory is already ours through Jesus Christ.

So here's the deal: Refuse to tolerate Jezebel. Don't let this insidious spirit have a seat at your table and interfere with your marriage. Stand firm in the authority God has given you.

Remember, this is where the curse ends and the blessing begins! Families will be restored. Marriages will be healed. Generations will rise up under the banner of God's covenant love.

Guarding What Is Sacred

Let's bring this home. Faithfulness means choosing to love when it's hard, choosing to forgive when it hurts, and choosing to honor your spouse even when you feel as if he or she doesn't deserve it. It means fighting for unity, standing against division, and saying, "*Not in my house!*" when the enemy tries to sneak in.

God is serious about marriage, and we should be too. He's not asking for perfection; He knows we will make mistakes. But He is asking for faithfulness, for a commitment to fight for the covenant, and to keep those spiritual doors to the demonic firmly shut. When we do that, we're not just protecting our marriage; we're building a legacy of blessing that will ripple through generations. And that, my friend, is worth fighting for.

KINGDOM REFLECTIONS

1. From the beginning, marriage was God's idea. He officiated the first wedding in the Garden of Eden and created marriage so that Adam and Eve would be united in spirit, soul, and body—and in covenant.
2. A covenant is no casual contract. It's a sacred, unbreakable bond anchored in God's unchanging nature and unwavering faithfulness. It reflects His commitment in the strongest possible way and is the foundation He laid for marriage.
3. Faithfulness in marriage is much more than not cheating. It's about guarding your words, your attitudes, and

your actions. You honor your marriage covenant not just with your body, but with your whole being—your heart, your mind, your words, and your behaviors.

4. Marriage is sacred, and it's worth fighting for—not just for your sake, but for the sake of future generations. It's the foundation for generational blessings, the construct on which legacy is built or broken.

5. Legacy and generational blessings are so important to God that He assigned the ancient prophet Elijah to facilitate them on the earth. The spirit of Elijah is on assignment to turn the hearts of families toward each other. Consequently, a demonic spirit typically known as Jezebel (or the great harlot) is on assignment to destroy marriage and covenant.

KINGDOM QUESTIONS

1. What is a covenant, and what are its foundations? Why is the concept of marriage woven throughout God's eternal story line, from beginning to end?

2. Why is human sexuality sacred for God's followers and significant in the eyes of God? Why does God take our sexual conduct so seriously?

3. How is faithfulness in marriage more than not cheating on your spouse?

4. What makes marriage sacred and worth fighting for? Who and what are counting on you to stay in your marriage?

5. How is the battle for marriage and legacy a spiritual matter? Is it strange to you that God would assign an ancient prophet to preserve families?

EIGHT

Breaking the Curse Brings Economic Revival

When the Holy Spirit prompted me to create a five-session course called *Keys for Supernatural Finances*, I knew it might challenge some people—and even ruffle a few demons along the way. I kept the price very low to remove any doubt of my intentions. I clarified that this wasn't a money-making ploy, but a ministry tool. The course was exactly what I said it was: a biblical teaching on prosperity, with a special focus on breaking financial iniquity, which are those generational strongholds that keep families trapped in cycles of lack.

The first four sessions? Smooth sailing. No drama, no distractions. But that final session on financial iniquity? Whew. I tried recording it twice, and both times, it just didn't sit right. I said to myself: *You'll have to do this one live*, but I was not expecting what came next.

The day of the live session, I grabbed my keys to head into my house. I kid you not—one of my house keys had folded clean over on itself, bent at a full right angle without my doing a thing. Yes, you read that correctly: *It bent by itself.* This wasn't some subtle *Did I imagine that?* moment. It was warped right there on my key ring! This was my only key from the garage to get into my house, and when I gently pushed it into the lock, it snapped. Just like that. Thank God my husband was inside and could let me in, because let me tell you, the enemy was already working overtime. By the way, this was a manifestation of sorcery, only I didn't understand it then.

It didn't stop there, either. As I set up for the live session in the studio at church, an actual demon *walked into the room just seconds before I went on air*. This wasn't a faint impression or a shadow in the corner. This spirit strutted right in, bold as brass, and stood there as if it could intimidate me. *Excuse me? No, sir.*

I had less than thirty seconds before going live, so I fired off a quick prayer request via text, looked that demon in the face, and then bound it in Jesus' name. I did this according to what Jesus told us in Matthew 18:18: "Assuredly, I say to you, whatever you bind on earth will be bound in heaven, and whatever you loose on earth will be loosed in heaven." I said something like this: "Devil, I bind you from operating right now, in Jesus' name. Get out now!"

And it left, of course. Because when the name of Jesus is involved, demons don't get to argue. And you know what? That session was fire. The anointing was heavy, and I knew the Holy Spirit was backing me up.

It was in that final session where financial iniquity and everything connected to it were boldly confronted and crushed. God hates poverty and has made a way out of it for all of us. Wouldn't you agree that poverty is both a mindset and a deeply spiritual issue? It's also underpinned by two factors: demonic influences that keep people bound, and land that has come under a curse. We will address both in this chapter.

To reiterate, generational iniquity and demonic oppression go hand in hand. This goes back to our discussion about strongmen and strongholds, and if you want to walk in true financial freedom, both must be confronted and broken. Also, the second factor—land under a curse—might challenge some perspectives, but it is grounded in Scripture. We'll need to dig into this with an open heart and a willingness to align with God's Word, as it is definitely a topic out of our comfort zone. Let's break these factors down.

Secret Oaths, Symbols, and Spiritual Ties

Let me take you back to a peculiar chapter in my city's history—a time when you couldn't even land a job at a particular long-standing organization unless you mentioned your affiliation with Freemasonry or boldly flashed your Masonic ring during the interview. If you were "in the club," you were the first to be hired and fast-tracked to job security, generous pay, and a cushy pension. But for those on the outside looking in, it left you wondering, *Is this just a club, or is it a cult?* After everything I've seen and experienced, I'm telling you that it's the latter.

In his handbook on cults, scholar and theologian Dr. Ron Rhodes describes Freemasonry as "a centuries-old fraternal and secret society deeply entrenched in symbolism, secret oaths and secret rituals."[1] Some people are lured in by the mystique of hidden knowledge. Others are drawn to its so-called humanitarian philosophy or the promise of brotherhood. And let's be real— some just want the business connections. But here's the hard truth: You cannot call Freemasonry a Christian organization. Why? Because there is *nothing*—absolutely *nothing*—of Christ in Freemasonry.[2]

We've all seen the symbols, the secret handshakes, the "G," and the compass.[3] History records plenty of well-known Masons—European royalty, United States presidents (at least fourteen of them), prominent thinkers, inventors, and even actors. They've left their fingerprints all over history.[4] And yes, Freemasonry has made significant contributions to society. Freemasons are known for their charitable giving, especially in caring for widows and orphans within their own ranks.[5] For those in the first three degrees, it seems like just a moral and fraternal organization focused on good works. Many Masons even argue that it's nothing more than that, especially when Christians start asking the hard questions.

But that's just the surface level. Those who have climbed the ladder—who've broken their blood oaths of secrecy to expose what's really going on—tell a different story. The higher degrees (there are thirty-three of them) pull back the curtain on a foundation built on paganism, reflections of white witchcraft, and eerie parallels to Qabalah (Jewish mysticism). And here's where it gets real: In the highest degrees, a belief emerges that Lucifer isn't the enemy, but a *benevolent* being—an equal to God—whose supernatural energy must be harnessed and applied.[6]

This is where discernment is critical. When you filter Freemasonry through the lens of Scripture, its deeper layers reveal something far more spiritual—and far more sinister—than what appears on the surface. This is not just an innocent, good ol' boys' club with a few quirky traditions. This is an occult system, and it carries real spiritual consequences.

I've noticed something over the years: Families tied to Freemasonry often carry a cluster of curses, like a storm cloud that just won't clear. The most glaring of these? *Financial collapse.* Patterns of dwindling resources and generational poverty that seem almost impossible to break. Why? Because Freemasonry, like every occult system, connects you to a source for power and provision that is not God. And when you yoke yourself to the wrong source, you invite the wrong spirits. As I've taught repeatedly through these chapters, iniquity will bind generations to familiar spirits until someone deals with it.

The Bible is clear: *Every* good and perfect gift, including financial provision, comes from God (see James 1:17). God has laid out a divine blueprint for supernatural prosperity—one that flows through the power of covenant and obedience. When we honor Him with the full tithe, sow generous offerings, and walk in alignment with His commands, we unlock the windows of heaven. His blessing isn't just financial; it overflows into every area of our lives, releasing favor, protection, and divine increase! And guess what? Our children and grandchildren will reap the blessing when we walk in obedience! It's right there in Scripture. Hebrews 7:9–10 tells us that Levi was credited with Abraham's tithe to Melchizedek *before he was even born!* That's how powerful doing finances God's way is. It marks our children for blessing and favor.

Sadly, when people reject God's ways, they start looking for alternatives—whether it's hustling in their own strength, joining secret societies, or straight-up making pacts with demons for financial gain. This isn't just bad decision-making. It's *iniquity.* And iniquity triggers a cycle of cursing—specifically a financial curse—that repeats generation after generation *until someone rises up and breaks it.*

So here's my question for you: Is there Freemasonry in your family line, and have you seen these patterns play out? If so, it's time to get free. It's time to *break the curse.*

Prayers to repent of Freemasonry and renounce Masonic curses are typically wordy and lengthy because of this system's complexity and far-reaching occult effects. When you start taking steps to get free, take your time and ask for help from a qualified pastor or prayer counselor, if needed. In the endnotes, I provide some links that will take you to examples of prayers you can use to repent of and renounce Freemasonry and declare your freedom.[7]

The Layers of Darkness

Like all occult systems, Freemasonry has layers. Some layers seem harmless, or even benevolent, but make no mistake, they can get sinister really fast. I'll never forget a woman who approached me after a meeting, clutching my *Inner Healing and Deliverance Handbook*. She had read it, and now she needed to talk.

"My ex-husband won a government contract for business," she told me. "He began attending these secret meetings. He said it was Freemasonry and connected to the people he worked with."

What she described was beyond disturbing. She had been taken to these meetings and drugged, assaulted, possibly chipped, and hypnotically programmed "for future use." As her marriage unraveled, threats and paralyzing fear kept her silent. She tried to dismiss it as her imagination, but the evidence was hard to deny. After reading my book, she realized that those dissociated memories weren't confusion—they were real.

Now, let me be clear. I've met my share of people who were mentally unbalanced and spouting wild conspiracy theories that didn't hold up. One woman was convinced that Satanists were after her, and she landed herself in jail after she mistook a police officer for one. This was not that. This woman who approached me was sharp, articulate, and highly professional—a businesswoman who carried herself well. But the trauma she had endured had left her dissociative, a heartbreaking but common result of abuse at the hands of malevolent groups.

Dissociation isn't some abstract concept. It's an actual, documented condition. When trauma is too much, the mind splits to protect itself. It's why some victims experience amnesia, feeling disconnected from reality, and even from their own identity. But here's the good news: Healing is possible. My book helped her start that journey, and I pointed her to further resources to go deeper.

I didn't say this at the time, but I knew part of this woman's healing would involve breaking the ritual curses connected to financial gain—the ones where she had been made an offering to demons, likely with no memory of it. It was a hard truth, but facing it would bring her personal freedom and disconnect her from any dangling financial curses. I know from experience that the Holy Spirit will bring this kind of thing to light in His timing too.

Incredibly Dark

Let's go back to the story I started with. Why did my key bend on its own that day? Why did that demonic presence manifest just before I addressed financial iniquity? These questions led me into a deeper journey with the Holy Spirit.

That demonic spirit was incredibly perverse and unclean, showing up right as I engaged in breaking financial iniquity during the course I was teaching. It was a familiar spirit—but why?

Around that time, buried memories started to surface. These were things I hadn't been able to remember before. In the *Inner Healing and Deliverance Handbook*, I shared about a ritual I began to remember as I slowly came out of dissociative amnesia, one horrific memory at a time. Dissociative amnesia is a trauma response. It's not regular forgetfulness. It's when your mind blocks out traumatic memories because they're too overwhelming to face. They stay hidden until healing begins to make it safe enough to remember.

I was a young teenager when I was forced into a pagan ritual that looked like a wedding. It happened in Southern California.

It wasn't a legal marriage. It was demonic, and I didn't understand what was happening. The trauma fractured my mind. I was left with only fragments and flashes. Yes, there were physical acts involved, although I didn't understand them then. The entire ritual was meant to destroy me at every level—spirit, soul, and body. But as healing came, the truth began to come into focus.

Here's what I remembered: The man was from Hollywood, a musician and a sorcerer. His mother was of Jewish ethnicity, small in stature, and unbecoming. She and my biological father had arranged for me to be sold into this ritual, but for what purpose? Even after months of deep healing work and therapy, something inside me still felt stuck. I couldn't find full resolution, and I struggled with a hidden resentment toward Jews. It didn't make logical sense; I knew better. And yet, my young mind had formed the association, and my adult heart was still caught in it. I couldn't uproot it on my own.

So I applied two biblical principles. First, Genesis 12:3—*if you bless Abraham, God blesses you*. Second, Matthew 6:21—*where your treasure is, there your heart will be also*. I began giving sacrificially to Jewish evangelism, directing my finances where I needed my heart to move.

Several months later, I had a disturbing dream. In it, I stuck a needle through my eyelid. When I woke up, I could still feel the sensation. Then the Holy Spirit spoke: *Your giving has broken through the lid*.

I took that as a sign that something was about to open up. Shortly after that, I suddenly *remembered*. The man's name. His face. Even snippets of conversation before that demonic sealing took place. Every detail I verified online—including his mother. Just to be clear, I have no physical evidence and nothing of my recollection that would hold up in court. But I don't need that. The Holy Spirit settled it for me. This ritual had been a demonic exchange of this man's offering to the powers of darkness to gain favor for his career in Hollywood. And it appeared to have worked.

Meanwhile, I had been left with a lingering curse that the Holy Spirit took careful steps to expose and deliver me from. Since then, I have witnessed powerful breakthroughs. It appears that a lid has been lifted.

Here's what I have learned: Breaking financial iniquity is a process. The strongmen behind it? Occult spirits, familiar spirits, perversion, and the spirit of Mammon—all intertwined. My open door to the demonic was unforgiveness, and complex trauma doesn't heal overnight. It requires intentionality, creating new pathways in the opposite direction. But when you are intentional about it, the breakthrough is undeniable.

As for that man? I'm settled, and it's all in God's hands now. You *can* heal from the worst of the worst. And when you do, financial iniquity will break too. Those familiar spirits will lose their grip on you.

Healing the Land

Unbelievable. My friend was scheduled to minister at a conference, and the moment she walked up to the building—*BOOM*—she saw it. An army of black flying insects crawling all over the outer walls, like something straight out of the book of Exodus. Neither she nor I had ever seen or heard of anything like it. She said it looked as if a full-blown plague had hit the area, but for some reason, it was heavily concentrated right there on that venue. She let me know what it was like to walk through those doors with a wall of creepy-crawlers to her right and to her left. Her skin was *crawling* just as much as they were, and so was mine just listening to her describe it.

The moment she stepped inside the building, her discernment *skyrocketed*. It was like an emotional roller coaster she hadn't signed up for—anger, sadness, more anger. She felt as if she were spinning, but didn't know why. As the conference went on, the picture became clear. It had to do with spiritual defilement tied to the land and leadership, which I won't go into a lot of detail about here. But we both agreed—the swarm outside was the first red flag. Why? Because what happens in the natural often mirrors what is happening in the spirit.

You already know that I teach a lot about covenant. And we've talked about this before—disobeying God brings a curse. This goes all the way back to the Garden of Eden. Adam and Eve sinned, and what happened? God cursed the ground, which affected their provision, their work, and their *entire* existence:

> Then to Adam He said, "Because you have heeded the voice of your wife, and have eaten from the tree of which I commanded you, saying, 'You shall not eat of it':
> "Cursed is the ground for your sake; in toil you shall eat of it all the days of your life."
>
> Genesis 3:17

The late minister and author John Sandford said it best: "When man fell, land fell with him." And let me tell you, when you see something like that, you better start praying *fast*.

From Barren to Blessed

"If My people who are called by My name will humble themselves, and pray and seek My face, and turn from their wicked ways, then I will hear from heaven, and will forgive their sin and heal their land" (2 Chronicles 7:14).

We've heard this verse countless times at prayer meetings, revival gatherings, and calls to repentance. We understand the part about humbling ourselves, praying, and turning from sin. But what about the last part? *Heal their land*. What does that actually mean?

The answer is in the verse before it: "When I shut up heaven and there is no rain, or command the locusts to devour the land, or send pestilence among My people . . ." (verse 13). In other words, when a land is suffering—whether through drought, economic collapse, or widespread sickness—it's not just a physical issue. Something in the spirit needs to be addressed. And God gives us the keys: repentance and intercession. When we align with Him, what was broken begins to be restored.

I saw this firsthand in my own city. There was an utterly desolate area—no businesses, no development, just empty land. The Holy Spirit led us into an intense time of intercession for that region. I discerned a territorial spirit of witchcraft oppressing the land, and it was reflected in the barrenness of the area. Through prayer, fasting, and persistent spiritual warfare, we contended until that stronghold broke.

The result? Everything shifted. Businesses began moving in, jobs opened up, and the entire atmosphere changed. We even moved out there—a new home, a second church campus—because the land had literally transformed before our eyes.

God's promise to heal the land is more than just words. It's a reality for those who will stand in prayer and take spiritual authority. If you've been sensing stagnation or resistance over a region, maybe it's time to press in and see what's happening in the spirit. Because when breakthrough comes, everything changes.

The Land Remembers

In the beginning, God didn't just give Adam and Eve a garden to enjoy. He gave them dominion over the land. They weren't placed on earth just to exist; they were called to rule, steward, and bless it: "Be fruitful and multiply; fill the earth and subdue it; have dominion" (Genesis 1:28). But when sin entered, everything changed. Even the ground itself came under a curse: "Cursed is the ground for your sake; in toil you shall eat of it all the days of your life" (Genesis 3:17). When humankind fell, creation fell with it.

And here's the part many overlook: *The land still responds to sin.* Ever notice how some regions seem locked in cycles of poverty, natural disasters, or violence? It's not random. The land carries the weight of iniquity.

John Sandford put it this way: "Our sin is no private matter." What happens in secret leaves a mark. Sandford went on to say, "The state of our hearts is the state of the land on which we live."[8] Scripture confirms this again and again: "Even the land was defiled; so I punished it for its sin, and the land vomited out its inhabitants" (Leviticus 18:25 NIV).

This isn't just theory; it's a spiritual principle at work. In 2 Samuel 21, Israel suffered through a devastating famine that lasted for years. No rain, no crops, no relief. When David sought the Lord, God revealed the root issue: Saul had broken covenant with the Gibeonites, and the land itself was bearing witness against the injustice. Once David made atonement, the famine lifted. The land responded when there was true repentance.

We've seen modern-day examples of this too. Take Almolonga, Guatemala. This small village was once under the grip of a demonic deity that promised wealth but took lives in return. People who sold their souls to this spirit would receive supernatural riches until they hit their forties. Then their bodies would bloat painfully until they exploded, full of slithering, slimy worms. It was a literal curse.

Some courageous pastors refused to back down. They fasted. They prayed. They pressed in until heaven answered. When revival hit, everything changed. People were set free, healed, and saved. And then, something incredible happened—the land responded. Almolonga, once barren and cursed, started producing some of the largest and healthiest vegetables the world had ever seen. Scientists traveled from all over just to study the phenomenon. When the strongman was broken, the land flourished.[9]

Even bloodshed leaves an imprint on the earth. When Cain murdered Abel, God said, "Your brother's blood cries out to Me from the ground" (Genesis 4:10). We learn from Hosea 4:1–3 that sin and bloodshed in a region can even drive away the animals and fish. The land bears witness to human sin, and when there's unrepented bloodshed, stolen land, or broken covenants, it creates a spiritual economic resistance in a region.

If you've been sensing a heaviness over a region—whether it's economic stagnation, constant turmoil, or an inability to thrive—it's time to ask some deeper questions: *What's in the spiritual history of this land? What injustices still need to be addressed?* Because when we take spiritual authority, break the strongholds, and walk in repentance, the land has to respond.

Repentance Is the Divine Reset Button

Mother Basilea Schlink and her sisters learned firsthand how the land reacts to both iniquity and repentance. As they worked to establish a center for their evangelical sisterhood in post–World War II Germany, they kept hitting an unusual problem—a dump cart filled with sand kept derailing. Not once, not twice, but *six times*. Basilea received an unusual thought from the Holy Spirit that something in their attitudes had negatively influenced the physical world around them. So she called her sisters to repentance and reconciliation.

Do you want to know what happened next? The cart never jumped its tracks again, and a spiritual war move emerged in these Catholic sisters. Over and over, they witnessed this principle at work. They repented and prayed and saw torrential rains stop. They repented and fasted and watched frost and heat waves shift. Again and again, through simple acts of repentance, humility, and prayer, the natural world around them aligned with the purposes of God.[10]

God already spoke about this kind of thing in Scripture:

> On the day that I cleanse you from all your iniquities . . . the desolate land will be cultivated instead of being a desolation in the sight of everyone who passes by. They will say, "This desolate land has become like the garden of Eden."
>
> Ezekiel 36:33–35 NASB

> Her wilderness He will make like Eden, and her desert like the garden of the LORD.
>
> Isaiah 51:3 NASB

History also confirms this truth. In early seventeenth-century America, a severe three-month drought threatened the New England settlers. But when the Protestant pilgrims humbled themselves, repented of greed and indifference toward others, and prayed for nine hours, the heavens opened. Rain came, and the drought ended.[11]

Years later, the settlers' descendants faced another crisis. An extreme caterpillar infestation was destroying their crops. Once again, they turned to prayer. They repented of idolatry, self-sufficiency, and spiritual complacency. Instantly, the plague stopped.[12]

These stories aren't just relics of the past. They are prophetic invitations for today. The land is listening. The question is, *What is it hearing from us?*

Sick Land, Sick Body

Every time I minister at a church built on Native American land, I get the same unmistakable stomachache—one that makes it downright difficult to minister. It's not normal, and it's not random. It's a tell. So wherever I am, I start asking questions. Sure enough, I hear the same story again and again: The land was taken unjustly by the government, sold off, and there has been no reconciliation.

When that's the case, I counsel the pastors and intercessors to take action. Not just a quick "Lord, forgive us" type of prayer, but real repentance. If possible, reach out to the tribe, I advise, and make things right. And yes, that will involve both money and ministry. I have yet to hear back from a pastor who has followed through, but I know this is the remedy, and it would shift everything. Because here's the deal: If the land is sick, the church on it will be sick too.

Not every battle is just "personal warfare." Sometimes, it's a land issue. I remember a worship leader who was struggling. She was talented and anointed, but something wasn't clicking. The resistance around her was almost palpable. As I watched the situation unfold, the Holy Spirit gave me a word of knowledge. So I walked right up to her one time and asked, "Do you have Native American ancestry?"

She answered, "No."

For a second, I thought, *Maybe I missed it.* But I obeyed the Holy Spirit anyway. I pointed straight at the ground we were on and spoke to it: "Do *not* reject her. Do *not* spit her out! In Jesus' name!"

The moment I did that, she calmed down. The shift was *instant.*

Later, she went home and asked her family, and guess what? She found a different answer. *Yes,* she did have Native American in her bloodline. And I believe the unresolved iniquity in her bloodline and a generational spirit of rejection was creating resistance between the land and her. Until that was addressed, the land itself was rejecting her.

I've seen this same pattern in others. People move to a new region, and suddenly they're hit with sickness, oppression, or a spiritual heaviness they can't shake. Why? Because land dynamics *matter*. When land carries the weight of unresolved spiritual issues such as stolen land, bloodshed, and broken covenants, the land *remembers*.

The good news is that there's always a way forward. Repentance. Reconciliation. Restoration. When we deal with the injustice, the resistance breaks, and the land responds.

When the Land Is Blessed, Everything Changes

I once preached this very message in St. Helena, California. Two weeks later, a devastating fire tore through the region, consuming everything in its path—*except* St. Helena. That town should have burned, but it didn't. Why? I believe repentance had opened a spiritual covering of protection over it.

When disaster looms—whether it's fires, storms, floods, or earthquakes—our first response shouldn't be panic; it should *be* repentance. Healed land isn't swept away by hurricanes. It isn't devoured by wildfires. It thrives under the peace and provision of God.

I see this truth play out in our church all the time. People walk in, and two things happen over and over: They often get physically healed, and they experience financial breakthrough. Why? Because we live on *blessed* land. We've fought for this ground in prayer. We've repented for past sins. And God has answered.

If you're seeing unrelenting hardship—in your city, in your church, or even in your home—it's time to take spiritual inventory.

What's in the land?

What's in the history?

What's in your bloodline?

Ask God. Repent where needed. And watch the land *respond*.

If My people who are called by My name will humble themselves, and pray and seek My face, and turn from their wicked ways, then I will hear from heaven, and will forgive their sin and heal their land.

2 Chronicles 7:14

KINGDOM REFLECTIONS

1. Breaking financial iniquity is key to unlocking supernatural prosperity, but confronting it often stirs up intense spiritual warfare.

2. Many families tied to Freemasonry experience cycles of financial collapse because of the spiritual agreements made with ungodly powers.

3. God's financial system operates on covenant principles. Tithing, sowing, and obedience unlock supernatural provision and generational blessing.

4. The land itself can come under a curse due to bloodshed, broken covenants, and unrepented sin, causing economic and environmental stagnation.

5. Biblical and historical accounts prove that when the people in a territory repent and align with God, supernatural economic revival follows.

KINGDOM QUESTIONS

1. Have you ever experienced unusual resistance when trying to break free financially? Could this be spiritual warfare linked to financial iniquity?

2. Have you or your ancestors been involved in secret societies or occult practices? If so, have you specifically broken any financial iniquity through repentance and prayer?

3. How do you view tithing and sowing? Do you see them as biblical principles of covenant, or as optional financial practices?

4. Do you feel a stronghold over your land, home, or workplace? Have you prayed over it and sought the Lord about any spiritual history tied to it?

5. What does it mean to you that the land can respond to sin and repentance? How does this change the way you pray for your region?

EPILOGUE

You Were Made for This

You've made it this far, and that alone tells me something: *You were made for this.*

You were never meant to be another casualty of generational bondage. You were never meant to live under the weight of what your ancestors struggled with. The cycles, the patterns, the warfare—it *ends* with you. Because you, my friend, *are a cursebreaker.*

By now, you've uncovered the spiritual roots that have entangled your family tree. You've learned to discern ancestral iniquities, territorial spirits, and the hidden chains that have held entire bloodlines hostage for generations. More importantly, you've learned how to fight back—not just for yourself, but for those who come after you.

But here's what I need you to understand: *The battle doesn't stop here.* Breaking a curse is one thing. Maintaining your freedom is another.

Just as generational curses are persistent, so must be your commitment to guard the ground you've taken. The enemy doesn't just pack up and leave because you prayed once. He looks for open doors. He waits for moments of weakness, hoping you'll let your guard down and allow the cycle to restart.

That's why you must live in the power of continual repentance, renewal, and spiritual warfare.

- Stay saturated in the Word—because the truth will always override deception.
- Keep your prayer life fiery—because intimacy with God keeps you spiritually sharp.
- Stay connected to a healthy, Spirit-filled church—because isolation is where the enemy preys.
- Walk in holiness and obedience—because disobedience is an invitation for the enemy to return.

And never forget—your breakthrough wasn't just about you. The generations coming after you will inherit either your freedom or your bondage. Your children, your grandchildren, and their children after them will walk in either the blessings you secured or the battles you refused to fight. You have *shifted history* with your obedience. You have built a new foundation for your family—one of righteousness, blessing, and divine inheritance.

This is your legacy. And this is only the beginning. Now go forward, armed with the authority of Christ, the power of the Holy Spirit, and the assurance that *you are a cursebreaker*.

ACKNOWLEDGMENTS

First off, to my amazing husband and children: You are my rock, my joy, and my greatest adventure. Life with you is wild, wonderful, and full of laughter. Thank you for loving me, believing in me, and sticking with my nonstop flow. You are the real MVPs.

To my Harvest Ministries International team: Chantal, you are a powerhouse. Thank you for leading with excellence and endurance and for keeping everything moving even when I throw Holy Spirit curveballs at the last minute. To my staff: You make the impossible happen with style and grace. I could not do this without you.

To my executive pastors at Harvest Church—Pastors Alex, Elaina, and Alysia: You are bold, anointed, and a force to be reckoned with. I love running with you. And, Shelby, you are simply awesome. That is the only explanation needed.

A huge thank-you to my faith heroes—Bishop Dave and Mary Jo Williams, Dr. Michael Maiden, and Pastors Phil and Chris Pringle. Your wisdom, your fire, and your pursuit of the supernatural have shaped my life in ways I cannot fully describe. Thank you for setting the bar high and showing us the way.

And to every prayer warrior, encourager, and Holy Ghost troublemaker who has stood with me—this book would not be the same without you. I love you big.

Breaking Free from Generational Druidism

I attended a conference where for the first time, I heard a certain minister from Ireland speak. Her rhetoric carried the tone of a reformer, and part of her message was directed at national government. At one point, she led the audience in a prayer and said some things that caught my attention. I won't quote her prayer exactly, but she invited God to burn us alive as a living sacrifice until no flesh remained.

While her words were sincere and I understood her intent, they also gave me pause. Why? Because of what I had been studying about the Druids. Sacrifice by fire was historically a druidic practice. Additionally, the aspiration to control government was another one of their signatures. Let me be clear—I'm not suggesting that she had any connection to druidism, nor did I know anything about her background. Her phrasing and mentality, however, seemed to echo a deeply entrenched druidic influence—one woven so tightly into the fabric of her nation that it resonated in her communication that day.

The experience reminded me of how secretive and pervasive occult systems like druidism can be, subtly shaping people's mindsets and language even centuries later. It also confirmed my suspicions that we must address this more intentionally.

So then, let's dive into a crucial aspect of deliverance that can be quite shocking: breaking free from the chains of generational druidism. Often, people are surprised when they discover the impact of druidic influence in their lives. This revelation can hit hard because, while many have heard of the Druids, the true extent of someone's ancestral ties to these ancient practices might not surface until a deliverance process begins. The Druids were notorious for their secrecy, a trait that has kept their practices shrouded in mystery throughout history.

Even seemingly innocent customs like kissing under the mistletoe or making wishes by tossing coins into wells are rooted in druidic rituals. What seems whimsical on the surface masks the profound influence Druids had on society, wielding sorcery that has been subtly passed down through generations.

Druidism, with its deep roots in the Celtic tribes of ancient Britain, Ireland, and Gaul, stretched its reach into Western Europe long before the Roman Empire expanded its boundaries. Also known as druidry, this shamanic tradition bridged the natural and spiritual realms. Druids were revered for their knowledge of medicinal herbs and used them to heal, acting as mediators between humanity and nature.

But Druids didn't just connect with nature and venerate Celtic deities; they also practiced divination, augury, and interpreting omens to guide their communities. They wielded natural power, conjuring dense fogs and storms—a power that intrigued and sometimes unsettled Christian monks.

The true nature of druidic beliefs remains elusive because the Druids didn't write down their practices. Despite their education and access to written language, they relied on oral traditions to protect their sacred knowledge from misuse. This leaves us with only fragmented and often biased accounts from Roman and Greek sources, with the Romans particularly disliking the Druids due to their resistance to Roman expansion.

Some accounts suggest that Druids believed in the immortality of the soul and that the soul remained in the head even after death, until reincarnation. This might explain the practice of keeping the heads of the deceased, as they believed that people's souls were still in that part of the body. The loss of their oral traditions, however, means we may never fully grasp their precise beliefs.

Julius Caesar's writings, especially his *"Commentarii de Bello Gallico"* ("Commentaries on the Gallic War"), offer a rare glimpse into druidic life from a Roman general's perspective. These texts, penned between 58 and 50 BCE, provide some of the earliest records of Druid society, revealing their roles and spiritual practices.

Caesar described Druids as central to every aspect of Celtic life; they were priests, judges, historians, teachers, scribes, and poets. Their deep knowledge of Celtic mythology made them the keepers of both real and legendary histories, crucial to maintaining cultural continuity.

The Druids were considered extremely powerful in Celtic society and were basically untouchable. As the elite of the elite, they were granted sweeping exemptions—no taxes, no military duty, and being nearly above the law. Their influence was so profound that they could even excommunicate individuals from their faith, cutting them off from divine connection with the gods. Such excommunication wasn't just a spiritual setback; it marked people as unclean and led to their social ostracism. In essence, the Druids had a masterful grip on the fabric of society, shaping and controlling its very flow.

Druidic rituals sometimes involved dramatic acts of devotion, including human sacrifices. One vivid account describes a massive wicker "man" filled with animals, children, and adults being set ablaze as a collective offering. Other reports mention sacrifices by drowning, throat cutting, and stabbing, as well as the use of skulls and crossbones in rituals for divination, and possibly a cult of the head.[1]

Given these traditions, I've included some prayers for those seeking to renounce and repent from such generational influences. These prayers are vital, whether you live on land where Druids once practiced or you travel to areas where their influence might still linger.

Repentance Prayers for Generational Druidism

1. I renounce and repent of any ancestral involvement in druidic worship, sacrifices, or rituals.
2. I renounce and repent of any human sacrifices made by my ancestors, including those by burning, drowning, suffocating in cauldrons, and throat slitting.
3. I renounce and repent of any worship of druidic deities or animal gods by my forebears.
4. I renounce and repent of any ancestral practice of seeking guidance or decisions from the stars.
5. I renounce and repent of all forms of divination, personally and generationally.
6. I renounce and repent of tossing valuables into wells as prayers or offerings.
7. I renounce and repent of any familial allegiance to the high priest of the Druids.
8. I renounce and repent of generational sins of oppression by druidic orders over the peasant people.
9. I renounce and repent of generational sins of enslavement under druidic rule.

10. I renounce and repent of all family engagement in rites involving mistletoe, oak trees, acorns, or spirits associated with these elements.

11. I renounce and repent of any covenants made by my ancestors with water or river spirits (naiads).

12. I renounce and repent of the generational placement of human skulls or bones in buildings for ritualistic or decorative purposes.

13. I renounce and repent of any druidic control over land governance by my ancestors.

14. I renounce and repent of familial practices of wizardry, sorcery, witchcraft, and magic, including all associated items like staves, jewelry, hats, clothing, and potions.

15. I renounce and repent of the generational sin of stealing or borrowing the life force from any being—human, spirit, plant, or animal. I break all rituals, spells, chants, and curses that drain the life force from others.

16. I declare that the life force shall be restored to its rightful owner, as created by Jesus. I proclaim that no further generational theft of life force will occur, and my descendants and I shall receive all life given by God.

17. Lord Jesus, forgive my ancestors and me for seeking revelation through the psychic realm.

18. I declare that the blood covenant I have with Jesus supersedes all demonic and druidic covenants.

19. God, apply the blood of Jesus to cleanse both my family line and me from all sin, rebellion, and iniquity.

20. I ask You, Jesus, to cleanse my spirit, soul, mind, body, name, gift, and destiny.

21. Specifically, I ask You, Lord, to remove any residual label of "traitor," especially any implication of "high

treason" against civil leadership, from my bloodline and me.

In the name of Jesus, let every chain of generational druidism be broken, and Lord, let us walk in the fullness of Your freedom and light.[2]

Appendix B

We Decree the New

Decreeing the new is a core part of my prayer life, something I regularly bring before the Lord. I don't just hope for change—I *decree* it.

First, I ask God to devour every familiar spirit with His holy fire, just as He instructed me. These spirits thrive on focusing on the past, keeping people bound to old cycles, old relationships, and old limitations. They resist the new, but they don't get to stay.

Next, I seek the counsel of the Holy Spirit and ask, *Am I holding on to anything or anyone from the past that is blocking the new thing You have purposed for me?* Because sometimes, we're the ones clinging to the familiar when God is trying to lead us forward.

Finally, I don't just wait for the new; I decree it into my life. I open my mouth and declare and decree, *God is doing a new thing!* I then begin to call in the new, speaking it into existence with authority and expectation.

Now it's your turn. Take this list of the new and make it personal. Declare it over yourself, your family, and your future.

Let your words shape the path ahead as you step into the new that God has prepared for you.

New additions

New and better counsel

New and better emotional stamina

New and better ministry invitations

New and better reputation

New and better vacations

New and better voices around me

New and enduring riches

New and profitable business

New and profitable properties

New and unusual miracles

New angelic visitations

New anointing

New appointments

New assignments

New authority

New beauty

New beginnings

New blessings

New boldness

New books

New breakthrough

New church campuses

New church plants

New connections

New conquests

New creativity

New deliverance

New depths

New direction

New doors

New dreams

New elevation

New encounters

New faith

New favor

New finances

New fire

New friendships

New fruit

New glory

New grace

New growth

New harvests

New health

New heart

New holiness

New houses

New impact

New increase

New influence
New innovation
New insight
New intercession
New investments
New joy
New knowledge
New mandates
New mantles
New maturity
New media
New messages
New mindset
New ministry
New miracles
New multiplication
New nations
New opportunities
New outreach
New places
New platforms
New podcasts
New power
New praise
New prayer
New promotion
New prosperity
New purity
New rain

New reconciliation
New relationships
New resolve
New rest
New restoration
New revelation
New salvations
New seasons
New signs
New songs
New spaces
New storehouses
New strength
New success
New teaching
New territory
New travels
New understanding
New upgrades
New utterances
New victories
New vision
New visions
New wealth
New wine
New wisdom
New wonders
New worship
New youth

NOTES

Chapter 1 Ancestral Spirits, Druids, and the Familiar

1. Daniel 10:20 reads, "Then he said, 'Do you know why I have come to you? And now I must return to fight with the prince of Persia; and when I have gone forth, indeed the prince of Greece will come.'" Ephesians 6:12 tells us, "For we do not wrestle against flesh and blood, but against principalities, against powers, against the rulers of the darkness of this age, against spiritual hosts of wickedness in the heavenly places."

2. Syed Rafid Kabir, "Druids: The Mysterious History of Ancient Druids, Their Religion, Gods, and Practices," History Cooperative, October 7, 2024, https://historycooperative.org/druids/.

3. Stuart Piggott, *The Druids* (Thames & Hudsen, 1999), 102, 110.

4. Jeremiah 3:8 states, "Then I saw that for all the causes for which backsliding Israel had committed adultery, I had put her away and given her a certificate of divorce; yet her treacherous sister Judah did not fear, but went and played the harlot also."

5. I included a similar version of this prayer in my *Inner Healing and Deliverance Handbook* (Chosen, 2022), 129.

6. Jesus told us, "Assuredly, I say to you, whatever you bind on earth will be bound in heaven, and whatever you loose on earth will be loosed in heaven" (Matthew 18:18).

7. Kimberly Daniels, *Breaking the Power of Familiar Spirits* (Charisma House, 2018), vii–viii.

8. Merrill C. Tenney, ed., *The Zondervan Pictorial Bible Dictionary* (Regency Reference Library, 1983), 275.

9. For more on this, see "What Is a Medium?," Got Questions, last updated January 4, 2022, https://www.gotquestions.org/what-is-a-medium.html.

10. Kynan Bridges, *Overcoming Familiar Spirits: Deliverance from Unseen Demonic Enemies and Spiritual Debt* (Whitaker House, 2022), loc. 225, Kindle.

Chapter 2 Understanding Strongmen and Strongholds

1. "Who Was Moloch?," Got Questions, last updated January 4, 2022, https://www.gotquestions.org/who-Molech.html.

2. For more information, see the article cited in note 1, "Who Was Moloch?"

3. This definition comes from Tony Evans, as related in Leighann McCoy's online article "Binding and Loosing: A Powerful Privilege and Responsibility for Us," The Prayer Clinic, August 9, 2023, https://www.prayerclinic.com/blog/binding-and-loosing-a-powerful-privilege-and-responsibility-for-us.

4. Dr. Jerry Robeson and Dr. Carol Robeson, *Strongman's His Name . . . What's His Game? An Authoritative Biblical Approach to Spiritual Warfare* (Whitaker House, 1984), 1. See also B. Childress, "Spiritual Warfare: The Sixteen (16) Strongmen listed in the Bible" (a list that doesn't include the spirit of poverty), Life in Jesus Ministries, August 22, 2008, http://lifeinjesus-ministries.com/SWSIXTEENSTRONGMEN.html.

5. For more on this, see Robeson and Robeson, *Strongman's His Name*, 157, 185, 132.

6. Derek Prince, "War in Heaven and Earth: Part 2—War on Earth," YouTube video, 7:31–7:55, posted by Derek Prince Ministries, April 7, 2015, https://www.youtube.com/watch?v=YPnLlA4SRoA.

7. I included this quote from Charles Kraft in my book *Seeing the Supernatural* (Chosen, 2017), 153. It originated in his book *Defeating Dark Angels: Breaking Demonic Oppression in the Believer's Life* (Chosen, 2016), chapter 2 (Myth 1), Kindle. You can also read more about the topic of Christians and demons in my online article "Can a Christian Be Demon Possessed?," available at https://www.jennifereivaz.com/can-a-christian-be-demon-possessed.

8. For more information on self-deliverance, see my article "What Is Self-Deliverance?," May 27, 2025, https://mailchi.mp/jennifereivaz.com/what-is-self-deliverance.

Chapter 3 You'll Break Through in This Generation

1. "4053.perissos," Bible Hub, accessed July 31, 2025, https://biblehub.com/greek/4053.htm.

2. Brian R. Doak, "The Canaanites," chap. 2 in *Ancient Israel's Neighbors* (Oxford Academic, 2020), abstract, https://academic.oup.com/book/33589/chapter-abstract/288065012.

3. Marilyn Hickey, *Breaking Generational Curses: Overcoming the Legacy of Sin in Your Family* (Harrison House, 2000), 22.

4. Hickey, *Breaking Generational Curses*, 23.

5. For more on this, see "Why did Noah curse Canaan instead of Ham?," Got Questions, last updated October 3, 2023, https://www.gotquestions.org /curse-Ham-Canaan.html. See also Don Stewart, "Why Was Canaan Cursed Instead of Ham?," Blue Letter Bible, accessed July 31, 2025, https://www .blueletterbible.org/faq/don_stewart/don_stewart_747.cfm. Likewise, see Hickey, *Breaking Generational Curses*, 26.

6. For more on this challenge, see "The Jebusites Inhabited Zion," Worship Warriors Ministry, accessed July 31, 2025, https://worshipwarriorsministry .com.au/how-david-took-the-stronghold-of-zion/.

Chapter 4 When You're the First to Break Free

1. Dr. Michael Maiden, preaching at Harvest Church, February 22, 2025.

2. For more on this, see Wikipedia, "William Brewster (*Mayflower* Passenger)," last updated April 2, 2025, https://en.wikipedia.org/wiki/William _Brewster_(Mayflower_passenger).

Chapter 5 The Power to Restore a Family Bloodline

1. *Merriam-Webster Dictionary*, "declare," accessed July 31, 2025, https:// www.merriam-webster.com/dictionary/declare.

2. Elizabeth Nixon, "Are You Decreeing and Declaring in Your Prayers?," *Charisma*, February 28, 2014, https://mycharisma.com/spiritled-living/prayer -devotion/are-you-decreeing-and-declaring-in-your-prayers/.

3. Several translations of Psalm 106:15 phrase *leanness* as a "wasting disease."

Chapter 6 Here Comes the New

1. Some information in this section is drawn from Dr. Sarah Pawlicki, "Aimee Semple McPherson," National Park Service, last updated March 19, 2025, https://www.nps.gov/people/aimee-semple-mcpherson.htm. See also *American Experience*, season 19, episode 10, "Sister Aimee," written, directed, and produced by Linda Garmon, aired April 2, 2007; Matthew Avery Sutton, *Aimee Semple McPherson and the Resurrection of Christian America* (Harvard University Press, 2007); Jim Hilliker, "KFSG Los Angeles—the Aimee Semple McPherson Station," Radio Heritage Foundation, February 17, 2006, https://www.radioheritage.com/story51/. Excerpts of McPherson's radio sermons are publicly available via the Internet Archive's "Aimee Semple McPherson Recordings," https://archive.org/details/Aimee -Semple-McPherson.

2. "US California Listings," Healing and Revival, accessed July 31, 2025, http://healingandrevival.com/USCA.htm.

3. Helen Alma Hohenthal, *Streams in a Thirsty Land: A History of the Turlock Region*, ed. John Edwards Caswell (Peninsula Lithograph, 1972), 239.

4. "What Does Genesis 38:29 Mean?," BibleRef, accessed July 31, 2025, https://www.bibleref.com/Genesis/38/Genesis-38-29.html.

5. For more on widows facing this kind of scenario in biblical times, see "Deuteronomy 25:5–10 meaning," The Bible Says, accessed July 31, 2025, https://thebiblesays.com/en/commentary/deu+25:5. There, we find this explanation: "Moses described the situation as *when brothers live together and one of them dies and has no son* (v. 5). The first thing that this law required was that *the wife of the deceased shall not be married outside the family to a strange man.* In this scenario, the widow was not free to marry anyone she wanted. Instead, *her husband's brother* was to *go in to her and take her to himself as wife and perform the duty of a husband's brother to her.* The brother of the *deceased* was supposed to respond positively to the plight of the widow by taking her as wife and engaging in sexual intercourse with her. Doing so would enable her to have a son to preserve the lineage of her *deceased* husband. This offspring would cause the property of the deceased lineage to continue in his line. In a sense then, the widow would inherit the brother's property and income from that property through the offspring given to her by the surviving brother."

6. For more on Perez, see "Who Was Perez in the Bible?," Got Questions, last updated January 4, 2022, https://www.gotquestions.org/Perez-in -the-Bible.html.

Chapter 7 Fight for Your Marriage

1. Dr. Dennis F. Kinlaw, *Let's Start with Jesus: A New Way of Doing Theology* (Zondervan, 2005), location 956, Kindle.

2. For more on this ministry of Elijah, see Dr. Jürgen Bühler, "The Restoration of All Things," International Christian Embassy Jerusalem, February 27, 2014, https://www.icej.org/blog/the-restoration-of-all-things/.

Chapter 8 Breaking the Curse Brings Economic Revival

1. Dr. Ron Rhodes, *Find It Quick Handbook on Cults & New Religions* (Harvest House, 2005), 112.

2. David Legge, "Strongholds Shaken—Part 14: 'Freemasonry,'" Preach the Word, May 2005, https://www.preachtheword.com/sermon/cults15.shtml.

3. For more on these symbols, see "Behind the Masonic Symbols: Square and Compasses," The Grand Lodge of Ohio, accessed July 31, 2025, https://www.freemason.com/masonic-symbols-square-compasses/.

4. For more on U.S. presidents who were Freemasons, see Tom Murse, "List of Presidents Who Were Masons," ThoughtCo., last updated May 8, 2025, https://www.thoughtco.com/presidents-who-were-masons-4058555.

5. For more on Masonic charity work, see "A Brief History of Masonic Charity," Pennsylvania Masons, November 29, 2017, https://pagrandlodge .org/brief-history-masonic-charity/.

6. Legge, "Strongholds Shaken."

7. Here are links to some prayers you can use to repent of Freemasonry and renounce Masonic curses, and to declare your freedom: https://media.web sitecdn.net/sites/727/20220929170123/prayerofreleasefreemason.pdf; https://www.godser.us/wp-content/uploads/2012/07/Deliverance-for-Freemasonry .pdf; https://luke-418.com/wp-content/uploads/Freemasonry-Renunciation .pdf.

8. John Sandford and Mark Sandford, *Healing the Earth . . . A Time for Change* (BT Johnson Publishing, 2013), 4.

9. There are several such stories, but this specific story about the curse on the land being broken can be found in Dave Williams, *The Road to Radical Riches: You Are Destined for Outrageous Wealth* (Decapolis Publishing, 2001), chapter 3, Kindle.

10. Mother Basilea Schlink, *Repentance: The Joy Filled Life* (Bethany House, 1968), 67–68.

11. Peter Marshall and David Manuel, *The Light and the Glory* (Fleming H. Revell, 1977), 142.

12. Marshall and Manuel, *The Light and the Glory*, 217.

Appendix A Breaking Free from Generational Druidism

1. Some of the information on Druids in this appendix was gathered from these resources, where you can also read more: HistoryNavigator, "The Power of the Druids," *Travel Through Time: Allison's History Blog*, October 21, 2017, https://historynavigator.org/2017/10/21/the-power-of-the-druids; Syed Rafid Kabir, "Druids: The Mysterious History of Ancient Druids, Their Religion, Gods, and Practices," History Cooperative, October 7, 2024, https://historycooperative.org/druids/; Brian Cox, "Toxic Waste from the Family Line—Celts and Druids," Aslan's Place, September 10, 2015, https://aslans place.com/language/en/toxic-waste-from-the-celts-and-druids/.

2. For further specific prayers to repent of and renounce druidism and its practices, see Brian Cox, "Prayer for Renunciation of Generational Druidism," Aslan's Place, June 26, 2013, https://aslansplace.com/language/en /prayer-for-renunciation-of-generational-druidism/. Likewise, see also "Generational Druidism," Kanaan Ministries, accessed July 31, 2025, https://www .kanaanministries.org/wp-content/uploads/2019/02/Druidism-Prayer-1.pdf.

JENNIFER EIVAZ is a minister, bestselling author, and international conference speaker with a deep passion to equip the Church in the supernatural. She is known for activating believers in healing, deliverance, and intercession, and for raising up prayer warriors who are both Spirit-led and biblically grounded.

She and her husband, Ron, pastor Harvest Church in Turlock, California. The church now meets in several locations and hosts a vibrant online campus that reaches people around the world. Jennifer also hosts the popular podcast *Take Ten With Jenn* and co-hosts *Navigating Church Leadership* with Ron. They are the proud parents of two wonderful children.

Jennifer has written several bestselling books, including *The Intercessors Handbook*, *Seeing the Supernatural*, and *Inner Healing and Deliverance Handbook*. She is a regular contributor to leading Christian media outlets and has been featured on multiple television programs. Her teaching is marked by depth, clarity, and a strong prophetic edge that calls the Church to walk in maturity and power.

You can stay connected with Jennifer and access resources through her website and social platforms. She shares regular prophetic insight, spiritual equipping, and updates from her ministry around the world.

Connect with Jennifer:

JenniferEivaz.com

@JenniferEivaz   @PrayingProphet

@PrayingProphet   @JenEivaz